Read to Me!
Read to Me!

A Guide to Reading Children's Literature Aloud

Written by Ina Massler Levin, M.A. and Michael H. Levin, M.A.

Illustrations by Ken Tunell

Teacher Created Materials, Inc.

Teacher Created Materials, Inc.

6421 Industry Way

Westminster, CA 92683

© 1998 Teacher Created Materials, Inc.

Made in U.S.A.

ISBN #1-57690-360-5

Library of Congress Catalog Card Number: 97-062340

Editor:

Janet Cain

Table of Contents

Table of Contents *(cont.)*

Table of Contents (cont.)

Introduction

"Read to me! Read to me!" How often we hear these words from our children whether we're parents, grandparents, or teachers. Young children love hearing the written word read aloud. And why shouldn't they? Stories are wondrous things for both young and old alike. Where else can you travel around the world, meet amazing people, laugh until you cry, and learn all sorts of new things without ever leaving the comfort of your easy chair?

A book in a child's hands can open new worlds for both of you. Reading is an activity that you can enjoy together. It is a portable pastime which can be accomplished comfortably in just about any place, including the living room, under a tree, at a park, in a classroom, at the library, or in bed. Stories passed from generation to generation also serve as a link to the past and a way to begin moving into the future. A love of reading will influence every part of your child's future education.

Reading aloud is also a lovely way to spend time with your child. In this very busy world, books force us to slow down. Their stories compel us to take our time as we read them aloud. Each age group has its own special way of listening.

Research reports from Johns Hopkins University suggest that reading to children as young as eight months helps set the beginning patterns for language development, even if they do not appear to understand. Nursery rhymes and poems are fun and easy to read aloud to babies.

Toddlers love to listen to stories—albeit for a very short time—about animals and other little ones their age. They'll be excited by the pictures while beginning to make the connection between the spoken word and the printed one. Three- and four-year olds will listen intently. They love turning the pages often before you tell them it's time. They will ask for the same story over and over again, memorizing certain parts or words and repeating them to you.

Introduction *(cont.)*

Beginning readers will relish pointing out words that they already know and may even read whole lines to you. They will listen and often correct you if you forget a word or leave out part of the story. Not only do they enjoy hearing stories from books, but they also take great pride in reading stories that they have written in school or with you. Beginning readers need lots of books they can read on their own.

Older children will be active listeners. They will ask sophisticated questions. Pay attention because they may surprise you. Often older children have favorite kinds of books. These may be about specific subjects such as dinosaurs or famous people. Sometimes it is fun to let them read books to you, especially those they might have listened to countless times when they were younger. Although this book doesn't deal with chapter books, there is no reason why you should not try reading some simple ones to your child, especially if he or she seems ready to listen. Chapter books are terrific for shared reading as your child matures.

Reading aloud is a wonderful family activity. Although reference is made in the **Ideas and Activities** sections to one child, stories can and should be shared with the whole family. Younger siblings can easily be included when reading books that appeal to older children. Just don't expect them to listen to the whole book. Parents may wish to take turns reading the same book. Older siblings might want to read to younger ones. The habit of reading aloud daily should begin early, when children are babies, and should continue even as children get older.

Yet how many times can you hear the same story? Your child will decide on some favorites and want to hear nothing else. For many children, the same books become part of the bedtime ritual. If your child insists that you read "that book" one more time, try being patient and using the tips in this book to make the reading more exciting. If your child is very young, you might be able to paraphrase or simply skip a few pages. However, this usually doesn't work for very long.

Consider it a compliment when your child loves hearing you read the same story over and over again. Remember, you are helping to create a lifelong reader, one who will pick up a book and enjoy it. You are also doing some other very important work. You are creating memories that will last a lifetime.

How to Use This Book

How you read stories to children can make a big difference in their involvement and reaction. It can also make a difference to the reader. The purpose of **Read to Me! Read to Me!** is to help make the process of reading to children an enjoyable and lively one for both the reader and listener. By giving hints on ways to read stories, topics to talk about, and activities to follow up with after reading, adults do not have to fear or dread reading aloud. This will be especially true when the plaintive cry of "More!" is heard. Parents, grandparents, teachers, and others who read to children will be able to appreciate their involvement.

The stories suggested in this book are ideal for an adult to read and discuss with a child. This kind of activity helps the child succeed in school, reinforces the emotional bond between the adult and child, encourages the child's natural desire to learn, and tells the child that reading is an important way to spend one's time.

Activities to enhance each story will help strengthen your child's connection to that book and add another element of fun to the reading. The types of activities range from very simple ones, which are appropriate for very young children, to those that will be accomplished only by older children. You will need to determine which are developmentally appropriate for your child. If you try an activity and it doesn't seem to work or your child lacks interest, put it away for another time. The most important interaction has taken place—you've shared the book with your child.

Locating the Books

The recommendations for each individual book are referenced in the following way:

author, title, illustrator, publisher, and copyright date.

This information is given so you can share it with your child and to make the book easier to locate. See page 11 which tells about sources for books. Sometimes two copyright dates appear. This is to give the reader an idea of the age of the book. Many stories have been around for decades. Do not let that deter you from reading the book. These stories are timeless. However, you might need to give a little more explanation for an older book since there may be words your child doesn't know or unfamiliar things shown in the pictures. Use this as a learning opportunity to point them out.

A list of various Web sites that will give you ideas and resources for expanding the world of reading is located on page 13.

Summary

Each story has a brief summary. This is to let you know what the story is about. It will come in handy when choosing stories, especially if you are trying to find a story about a specific topic or character.

How to Use This Book (cont.)

Hints for Reading Aloud

While general **Tips for Reading Aloud** are described on page 10, additional hints that are specific to each story are also provided. They will vary from book to book but when followed (even if they make the reader feel strange or silly) can add a great deal of interest and excitement to the story.

What to Talk About

Sometimes all that is required to read a book to a child is to read it. At other times, especially when you read the story over and over again, it will be a book that needs some discussing. The topics and questions in this section will give you some ideas for ways to take this particular story further. This section may prove very helpful when there is something in a story that your child finds confusing or upsetting.

Ideas and Activities

In this section, you will find a potpourri of activities that you and your child may wish to complete. Some are very simple, such as finding new words or tasting something that is mentioned in the story. Others are more complex, such as planting a vegetable garden or figuring out some math problems that relate to the story. Before attempting an activity, be sure to read through it since some do require specific materials or a minimal amount of preparation. Most of the activities cannot be accomplished alone. They are intended to help strengthen the adult-child relationship by encouraging mutual involvement.

Related Reading

In this section, you will find a short bibliography of stories that relate to the one you have just read. The relationship to the book you have read may be that (1) it is one in a series, (2) there is more information about the topic(s), or (3) there are other books by the same author.

Appendix

Here you will find ways to make books with children (pages 150–152), illustration award winners (pages 153–155), titles of beginning chapter books to read with your child (page 156), and lists of big book versions and titles of stories that are considered to be predictable (page 157).

Index

This index is divided into various categories to help you select books that you might want to read for a special reason. For instance, if your child is just beginning preschool, you might enjoy reading **Cleversticks** by Bernard Ashley (Crown, 1991), or if someone you know has just passed away you might want to read **Everett Anderson's Goodbye** by Lucille Clifton (Henry Holt and Company, 1983).

Tips for Reading Aloud

A Few Beginning Thoughts

- Children learn to listen by listening. Begin reading aloud when your child is still an infant. Your baby will get to know the pleasing sound of your voice as you read. Before you realize it, he/she will be listening to entire stories. Your child will look forward to the time you share reading together.

- Both the reader and listener should be able to see the book. Make it easy for your child to see the pictures. Always make reading a comfortable experience for your child as well as for yourself.

- There is nothing wrong with occasionally reading above your child's intellectual level. Studies show that this is a way to challenge a youngster's mind. However, be careful about reading above your child's emotional level. Reading should not frustrate the child's understanding of the world.

- It is a good idea to preview the book before you read it aloud. If you think your child might be frightened by the story, don't read it. As a parent, you get to choose the stories you think are appropriate.

- The debate over the damage caused by watching too much television is long and tiresome. As a parent, you have the right to restrict the amount of time your child spends watching television. Don't make your child choose between reading with you or watching a television program. If one of your rules is that the television is turned off by 8 pm, then bedtime reading becomes part of your daily schedule. Your child will learn that your house is a place where nothing takes the place of reading.

- A special note to fathers: It is very important for you to read to your sons and/or daughters. Your children need to know that learning and reading are activities enjoyed by men and women. You may see yourself playing sports with your sons and/or daughters, but they need to see you as a mentor for their educational pursuits as well.

As You Sit Down to Read

- Read at a comfortable pace. When reading aloud, a very common mistake is to read too quickly. As you read, your child is creating mental pictures. You need to allow enough time for that. Adjust your pace to fit the situation. If this is the twentieth time you've read a particular book, you can go a bit more quickly than if it's the first or second time.

- Use a great deal of expression in your voice. Try to give each main character its own distinctive sound.

- If reading aloud to your child feels strange or uncomfortable, try to relax. Reading aloud is a learned behavior. The more you do it, the better you will become. If your child enjoys it, you are doing very well.

- If your child is getting restless or isn't enjoying a particular book, you are under no obligation to finish it. Pick another. Both of you should be enjoying the experience.

- If your child cannot sit still while you are reading, provide some crayons and paper. Allow your child to draw as you continue reading.

- You will find many more tips specific to each book in the **Hints for Reading Aloud** section that follows the summary.

Where to Find Books

Where does one find books to read? There are many sources. Some will prove easier to access than others.

Libraries

The easiest place to find books for your child is at the public library. The library has books that are old and new, ones you have heard of and ones you haven't. Choose a few to read aloud to your child. Try to select ones that will hold both your attention and your child's. Allow your little one to choose a few books as well. The children's books are often located on low shelves so that even the youngest library patrons can reach them. If your library is fortunate enough to have a children's librarian, ask her/him for suggestions. Your local library may also have a story hour for children. If possible, give your child the opportunity to attend. This may provide you with some ideas for books that you and your child will enjoy reading at home.

Bookstores

The library is a wonderful resource with the advantage that the books are free. The downside is that you have to return the books. Chances are that you will want your child to have her or his own book collection. There are countless bookstores across the country. Some communities have children's bookstores staffed with people who have a wealth of information about children's literature. Many large bookstores have special children's sections. In some bookstores, you will find shelves that have employees' favorite books.

In bookstores you will also find many related products to go along with books. A doll which is the character in a book can be a special friend for your child. Bookstores also do promotions for books with authors coming for book signings so your child can meet published authors.

Secondhand Bookstores

In some communities there are secondhand bookstores. Some of these stores work on a barter system where you trade books, or you can buy the books. In other stores, there is no trading; you can simply buy the books. Secondhand bookstore prices are usually lower than retail bookstore prices, but newer titles may be more difficult to find.

Garage Sales

A treasure trove of inexpensive books can often be found at garage sales. Many people are anxious to get rid of books their children no longer read. Be sure to check the books before buying them to be sure all the pages are there.

Where to Find Books (cont.)

Schools

Many schools have fund-raisers where they sell books to children to earn money for the school. They may send home fliers in advance so you and your child will know what is available to buy. Often schools have books on their lists that are appropriate for the whole family so everyone can take advantage of the sale.

Gifts

When someone asks what to give your child as a gift, you can always suggest a book. Whether you recommend specific titles is up to you. If you are in charge of a children's gift exchange, suggest that everyone bring a book to trade. Here you may want to set a price limit.

Book Clubs

At some point, you may receive an announcement in the mail for a book club. Don't overlook this opportunity as a way to build up your child's library. Each book club has its own terms of membership, but most offer a wide selection of choices. One advantage of joining a book club is that you can choose the books you want to purchase while sitting in your home and have them delivered to your door.

The Internet

You can locate stories to read aloud using the Internet. Some addresses are suggested on page 13. As with any Internet activities, adults should supervise children when they have access.

Making Your Own Books

Children love to read books they have made. As they enter school, they will make big and little books to bring home. Before this time, you should make books with them. There are some suggestions for ways to make books with young children on pages 150–152. Add these books to your child's collection, or use them as gifts for family members.

Book Recommendations

There are many sources to get recommendations for books to read aloud to your child. **Jim Trelease's Read Aloud Handbook** is an incredible resource. **Horn Book Magazine** and **Booklinks** are just a few publications devoted to books. Many family magazines have book review sections as a feature. Review them to find ideas for new children's books to read aloud.

Read the book review sections in newspapers. Ask people you know for the titles of books their children enjoy hearing read. Playgroups, preschools, and elementary schools are excellent places to find out about new books.

Technology Connections

On this page you will find Web sites that you can visit to find some stories to read aloud.

Note: All of these sites were operational at the time that this book was printed. As with any Internet activities, be sure to supervise children if you allow them to have access.

Tales to Tell

http://www.thekids.com/kids/stories

This site has fables and stories from around the world.

Online Children's Stories

http://www.uclagary.ca/-dkbrown/stories.html

This site lists many other Web sites that take you to more reading for children.

Carol Hurst Children's Literature Site

http://www.Carolhurst.com

This site lists recommendations from picture books through young adult novels. Summaries and activities are given. Although it is geared to teachers, parents will also find information here.

Cyber-Seuss

http://www.afn.org/~afn15301/drseuss.html

This site leads to Dr. Seuss stories. It includes information about the author.

Multicultural Book Review

http//www.isomedia.com/homes/jmele/homepage.html

At this site, multicultural literature is reviewed by readers who submit reviews.

Reading Rainbow

http://www.pbs.org:80/readingrainbow/index.html

This site lists the titles that are shared on this popular read-aloud show. For each book a summary and an activity are given. Many of the books in **Read to Me! Read to Me!** appear here.

Children's Literature Web Guide

http/www.ucalgary.ca/~dkbrown/index.html

This site not only lists award-winning books but also provides links to other sites. Not only can you choose a story or book but also, in some cases, you will be taken to the text of that story.

Candlelight Stories

http://www.CandlelightStories.com

This site has a variety of stories you can print out and read aloud to your child. Some are wonderfully illustrated. There are also links that will take you to many other literature and reading-related sites.

Read Me a Story

http://www.visa.com

Once you arrive at this Web site, click on Read Me a Story. Here you will find some fabulous resources for reading aloud to your child. From favorite stories by the well-known and not-so-well-known authors to tips for reading aloud, this site will enhance the time you spend reading aloud to your child.

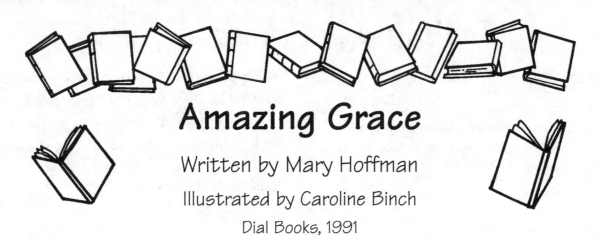

Amazing Grace

Written by Mary Hoffman

Illustrated by Caroline Binch

Dial Books, 1991

Summary

Grace is an elementary school student with a vivid imagination. Whenever she hears a story, she immediately acts it out with herself in the leading role. When she hears the teacher say that the class will present **Peter Pan,** Grace wants to play the role of Peter. Raj tells her it must be played by a boy. Natalie says Grace can't be Peter because she is black. She voices these concerns to her mother and grandmother, Nana. Nana takes her to see the ballet **Romeo and Juliet** with a woman from Trinidad as Juliet. Grace is so excited she tries out for the part of Peter. The other children vote unanimously for her. Grace is a great success and after the performance feels she "could fly all the way home!" Nana and Mother agree she probably could.

Hints for Reading Aloud

Make Nana sound like the voice of reason, especially after Mother becomes angry when she hears what Natalie said to Grace. Grace should be full of energy, only sounding sad when retelling what the students said to her about trying out for the part of Peter. This book should end on a high note with Nana's soaring ending words.

What to Talk About

- Discuss Grace's excitement about playing Peter Pan. Ask what part your child would like to play in a movie made from a book. Recount some of the movies and/or plays your child has seen which have appropriate roles for children.

- Discuss how the first few pages which show Grace's great imagination and love of performing lead to her wanting to play Peter. An older child can understand Grace's disappointment at the other children's remarks. Why do the other children say these things to Grace? Why does Natalie change her mind?

- What are the differences between a ballet and a play? How is a play different from a movie?

14

Ideas and Activities

- If your child has not been to a play, start looking for an appropriate one to attend. Your community might have a children's theater or a season of children's plays at a larger theater.

- If it is your child's first experience at live theater, pick a short play which she or he can sit through comfortably. It does not need to be a professional production. It is better to go to two or three community productions which would cost less than one with a professional cast.

- Besides the Walt Disney classic cartoon **Peter Pan** (Buena Vista Home Video), you might try to locate the musical version with Mary Martin (Good Times Home Video Corp.) as well as the brightly illustrated version of the original book by J. M. Barrie.

- This wonderful story lends itself to talking about equal opportunities for boys and girls as well as ethnic groups. If your child has begun to notice these differences, reemphasize the story's theme of equality by pointing out that all groups are an integral part of our modern society.

- With your child try "flying." You can pick up your small child and zoom him or her around. With your older child, you can spread your arms and "fly" around the room. What do you see from "up there"?

- Look for books with photographs taken from airplanes. There is a whole series of panoramic photo essays by Robert Cameron. (See the **Related Reading**.)

Show your child how everyday places look different from a bird's-eye view. You might have a young aviator right beside you.

Related Reading

Barrie, J.M. **Peter Pan.** Macmillan, 1990.

Bauch, Patricia M. **Dance, Tanya.** Putnam, 1989.

Cameron, Robert. **Above San Francisco II and Other Cities.** Cameron and Company, San Francisco, 1975.

Goldberg, Whoopi. **Alice.** Bantam, 1992.

Hathorn, Libby. **Freya's Fantastic Surprise.** Scholastic, 1989.

Hoffman, Mary. **My Grandmother Has Black Hair.** Dial, 1988.

Holabird, Katherine. **Angelina Ballerina.** Crown, 1988.

Ikeda, Daisaku. **Over the Deep Blue Sea.** Whitman, 1993.

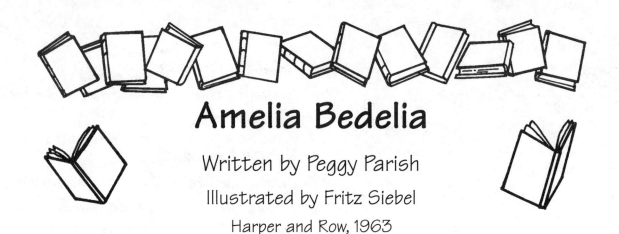

Amelia Bedelia

Written by Peggy Parish

Illustrated by Fritz Siebel

Harper and Row, 1963

Summary

Amelia Bedelia is beginning a new job as a housekeeper for Mr. and Mrs. Rogers. Although she has a long list of things to do, she decides to make a lemon-meringue pie first. Amelia Bedelia wants to do a good job with every task on the list, but she doesn't understand the directions that Mrs. Rogers has left. For example, she reads "dust the furniture" and proceeds to sprinkle dusting powder all over the living room. When told to "put the lights out" she unscrews all the light bulbs and hangs them out on the clothesline. She even puts overalls on dinner when told to "dress the chicken." The Rogers return home to a very different scene than they expected to find. Mrs. Rogers is about to fire Amelia Bedelia when Mr. Rogers gives her a taste of the pie. It is so delicious they decide to keep Amelia Bedelia and deal with her unusual ways.

Hints for Reading Aloud

Amelia Bedelia should sound confused when she doesn't understand Mrs. Rogers orders. Make her sound delighted as she carries out the tasks. Mrs. Rogers should be very angry upon returning home and then pleased after she tastes the pie.

What to Talk About

• Although the humor is obvious to you, your child might not understand some of it. Explain the double meanings of expressions called "idioms." After your child understands the humor, you'll both laugh every time you read it. Chances are you will receive frequent requests for this book.

• Ask your child whether Amelia Bedelia's mistakes are understandable. Relate times when you didn't understand what you were supposed to do and made mistakes as a result. Ask your child to remember a time when this happened to him or her.

• Ask your child to tell which of Amelia Bedelia's mistakes is the funniest and explain why.

Ideas and Activities

- If your child likes the humor in this story, you may wish to work together to create a list of idioms and puns. Humorous books can easily be found at the library.

- Has your child ever had lemon-meringue pie? If not, find a recipe and make one of your own or buy one readymade. After tasting it, ask your child whether or not he or she likes it. Does your child better understand Mr. Roger's reaction?

- Although it is not recommended that you let your child cut up the bathroom towels, he or she might like to "draw the curtains" or "measure the rice."

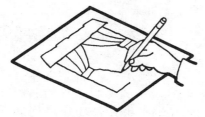

- Amelia Bedelia has a rhyming name. Think of other names that rhyme. Some of these might be legitimate names such as Rob Bob or May Faye. Others can be names such as Fancy Nancy or Like Mike. See if your child can think of words that rhyme with your names.

Related Reading

Abolafia, Yossi. **A Fish for Mrs. Gardenia.** Greenwillow, 1988.

Allard, Harry. **The Stupids Have a Ball.** Houghton, 1984.

Brown, Ruth. **The Big Sneeze.** Lothrop, 1985.

Freeman, Don. **Mop Top.** Viking, 1955.

Hilton, Nettie. **Dirty Dave.** Watts, 1990.

Mahy, Margaret. **Jam: A True Story.** Little, 1986.

Parish, Peggy. **Amelia Bedelia Helps Out.** Greenwillow, 1979.

Parish, Peggy. **Play Ball, Amelia Bedelia.** Harper, 1972.

Parish, Peggy. **Teach Us, Amelia Bedelia.** Greenwillow, 1977.

Wilson, Sarah. **The Day That Henry Cleaned His Room.** Simon & Schuster, 1990.

Bill McGill
Sue Balloo
Joe Blow
Terry Carey
Lora Nora

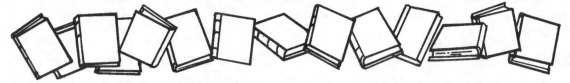

Anna Banana and Me

Written by Lenore Blegvad

Illustrated by Erik Blegvad

Atheneum, 1985

Summary

Anna Banana is a brave girl. She runs down hallways with shadows, goes "higher than high" on the swings at the park, flattens castles that she makes, and climbs on statues. Throughout Anna Banana's adventures a boy watches her. However, he is not able to be as courageous as she is. Anna Banana tells him that a feather is magic. His attitude changes greatly when a feather floats down for him to catch. By using it he conquers his fears and runs home.

Hints for Reading Aloud

Anna Banana is a little girl with a lot of pluck. She is adventuresome so make her parts sound full of bravado. She also seems to come with her own sound effects such as "Whooo-wheee!" When she makes these noises, read with great vigor. Also add the appropriate sounds for the parts when she is laughing or making echoes.

The narrator of the story is much quieter and more fearful than his playmate. Make him a timid character with a softer sounding voice. He should sound terrified as he is left with the goblin and relieved when he finds the feather. Have him laugh at the goblin.

What to Talk About

- Talk about a time when you were afraid and another time when you were brave. Invite your child to do the same.

Ask your child some or all of the following questions:

- What makes you feel afraid? What do you do when you're afraid?
- Can a feather really be magic? How do you know?
- Did Anna Banana really see a goblin, or was it the sun going down in the sky?
- Which adventure in this story would you most like to have? Why?

Ideas and Activities

- Anna Banana seems to run everywhere. Run with your child. You can run from tree to tree, or you can simply run around the block. Have races if you wish.

- Play in the sand together. Try to make a birthday cake with sand. Use ice-cream sticks, as the characters in the story did, to make the candles. Decide together if you should stomp on it when you are finished playing.

- Go to the park to use the swings. If your child is very young, you may need to hold him or her in your lap while you swing. Otherwise, offer to push your child. Exercise caution around the swings.

- Turn on some music and dance with your child. If a mirror is nearby, dance in front of it. Invite some friends or family members to dance with you.

- Create an echo with your child. Find a place where your voice might reverberate. This could be a long hall or a small enclosed space. Call out your name and see what you hear come back. If you can't find a spot to do this, just play an echo game with your child. Each time your child says something, repeat it back. However, be forewarned; this can easily get out of control with your child echoing everything you say.

- Let your child draw what she or he thinks a tomato-face goblin would look like. Give your child plenty of drawing paper and red crayons or markers to create the goblin. Have your child give the picture a title and then hang it in a place of honor.

- You can make an apple turkey by using feathers, an apple, a large marshmallow, a thin-tipped marker, and toothpicks. Packaged feathers are available at many craft, party, and toy stores. Simply stick the marshmallow onto one side of the apple, using a few toothpicks. Draw a face on the marshmallow. Then stick feathers into the other side of the apple for the turkey's tail feathers.

Related Reading

Alexander, Sally H. **Maggie's Whopper.** Macmillan, 1992.

Cole, Joanna. **Anna Banana: 101 Jump-Rope Rhymes.** Scholastic, 1989.

Jezek, Alisandra. **Mioli's Orchids.** Raintree, 1991.

Keats, Ezra Jack. **Maggie and the Pirate.** Macmillan, 1987.

Purdy, Carol. **Iva Dunnit and the Big Wand.** Dial, 1985.

Taylor, Mark. **Henry the Explorer.** Little, 1988.

Wallace, Ian. **Morgan the Magnificent.** Macmillan, 1988.

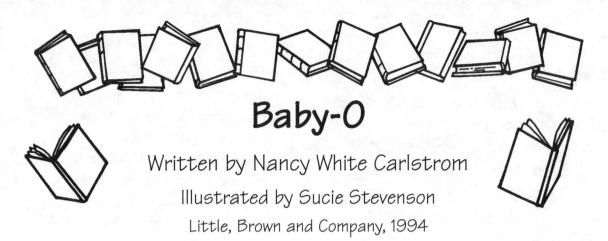

Baby-O

Written by Nancy White Carlstrom

Illustrated by Sucie Stevenson

Little, Brown and Company, 1994

Summary

Set in the West Indies, Baby-O is both the name of a jitney (bus) and the baby in the story. The jitney is on its way to the marketplace in town, and each member of the family brings something along on the bus. Besides the items that they bring, things like baskets, hats, and chickens, each person gets a special song. As the bus gets more and more crowded with people and things, the songs of the family sound longer and livelier.

Hints for Reading Aloud

This is an enjoyable book to read aloud because it uses the sounds the words can produce to enliven the story. With each character getting his or her own repetitive refrain, it will be a story to read with gusto. Many of the words such as "chuka," "wusha," and "pika" have strong sounds to them and should be emphasized as you read.

Although there is no music, this story is longing to be sung, at least in terms of reading it with musicality. Each family member in the story gets a line that begins with "Sing a song of . . . ," so try to give your voice a musical feel. The sounds, such as "plesh plesh," can be read in the same cadence as the rest of the lines when you read them the first time. Say them softly and slowly when the book shows words with many spaces between the letters.

If you read this with your family, let members take their equivalent parts in the song.

What to Talk About

Ask your child some or all of the following questions:

- Would you like to ride on the jitney with the family? Why or why not?
- Family members each bring along something that they have been involved in taking care of or producing. What would you want to take along?
- What does the family do when they get to town?
- Why do you think the baby and the jitney have the same name? Does the line "... watch it grow" have anything to do with this?

Ideas and Activities

- Make up a song for each member of your family. It can simply be sounds that go well together or slightly more elaborate. Sing it together for a holiday or other family get-togethers. You might even start a tradition.

- Mama-O hangs out her wash on a line. If your child has never done this, get a few clothespins and run a small line in a safe location such as over a bathtub. Let your child hang a few items, such as a washcloth or dishtowel, on it.

- In the story, the parents are Mama-O and Daddy-O, while the grandparents are Pappy-O and Granny-O. What does your child call you and the grandparents? Find out where people get the names they call their parents and grandparents. Do they use shortened forms of the names or terms from other languages?

- Sister-O eats mangoes that fall from the tree. Buy fresh or canned mangoes for your child to eat. Sometimes fresh mangoes are available in the produce departments of grocery stores. Be sure the mango is ripe before you peel and eat it.

- Plan an outing using the bus. You do not need to go far. Choose a less hectic time of day so you can get a seat by a window and point out what you see.

- Sing the song "The Wheels on the Bus." One source for this song and music is **Everybody Sings!** compiled by Debbie Coyle, DMC Publications, 1991.

- Granny-O weaves baskets using palm fronds. Invite your child to try weaving. Provide 1-inch (2.54 cm) wide strips from two different colors of construction paper. Cut these to any length you think your child can handle. Make at least eight strips of each color. To make this easy, take one strip of tape and at about 1 inch intervals, stick down one set of colored strips. Then show your child how to weave a strip of the other colored paper in and out. You may want to tape down the first weave.

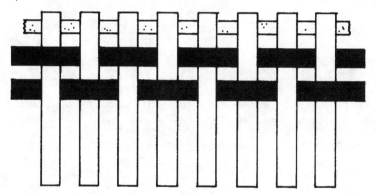

Related Reading

Binger, Kilty. **Mary Guy.** Lothrop, 1993.

Browne, Eileen. **Where's That Bus?** Simon & Schuster, 1991.

Daly, Niki. **Not So Fast, Songololo.** Macmillan, 1986.

Helen, Nancy. **The Bus Stop.** Orchard, 1988.

Hertz, Ole. **Tobias Catches Trout.** Carolrhoda, 1984.

Kingslad, Robin. **Bus Stop Bop.** Viking, 1991.

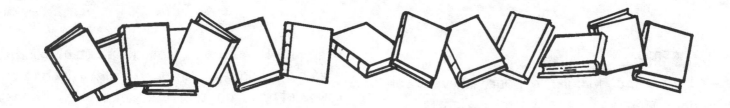

Bailey Goes Camping

Written and Illustrated by Kevin Henkes

Greenwillow Books, 1985

Summary

Bailey's brother and sister leave for a camping trip. Bailey is too young to go. Although Bailey's parents tell him that camping isn't very much fun, Bailey can see the truth of the matter. His parents try different activities to make him happy, but all he thinks about is camping. Suddenly, Bailey's mother realizes that he can go camping at home. He swims and fishes in the bathtub, tells scary ghost stories in the living room, plays in a sheet tent, and roasts marshmallows over the stove.

Hints for Reading Aloud

Make Bruce and Betty sound happy about going to camp so your child can see they are excited about the trip. Bailey's voice should be very sad when he tells his parents why he wants to go camping. This will help your child sense Bailey's unhappiness. Make Mama's voice very excited when she tells Bailey that he can go camping at home.

What to Talk About

- If your family has ever been camping, have your child tell about the experience and what she or he enjoyed the most.

- Was there anything unpleasant about camping which Bailey didn't have to deal with by doing it at home?

Ideas and Activities

- It might be fun for your child to do some or all of the camping-at-home activities shown in the book. If your child has never been camping, an overnight stay in the backyard might be just the ticket. If you prefer, you and your child can build an indoor tent by spreading towels or a sheet over a few chairs. Grab a flashlight and a book before crawling in. Then read aloud in this special spot.

- If you have a sporting goods store near you, explore the camping section. They might have a tent set up which you and your child could examine.

- Older children might be ready for a not-too-scary ghost story. You can make one up or find a book in the library. When telling ghost stories, take heed. Your child may really become frightened so determine if she or he can handle this experience.

- A day trip to a beach, lake, or park can end with roasting marshmallows. You may wish to improve on Bailey's experience by adding chocolate for a deliciously messy s'more. S'mores are easy to make. All you need is a graham cracker, 4 squares of a chocolate bar, and a roasted marshmallow. The marshmallows can be toasted in a microwave or over a barbecue grill, but they'll be sticky. Make a sandwich with the two halves of the graham cracker. Place the chocolate squares on half of the graham cracker. Then put the roasted marshmallow on the chocolate, and cover it with the other half of the graham cracker. They're better than delicious, and your child will soon find out why they are called s'mores.

- Look up in the sky one evening and do some star-gazing.

Related Reading

Carlson, Nancy. **Arnie Goes to Camp.** Viking, 1988.

Carrick, Carol. **Sleep Out.** Houghton, 1982.

Dauer, Rosamond. **Bullfrog and Gertrude Go Camping.** Dell, 1988.

Mayer, Mercer. **You're the Scaredy-Cat.** Rain Bird, 1991.

Roche, P. K. **Webster and Arnold Go Camping.** Puffin, 1991.

Schwartz, Henry. **How I Captured a Dinosaur; Amos Camps Out: A Couch Adventure in the Woods.** Little, 1992.

Tufuri, Nancy. **Do Not Disturb.** Greenwillow, 1987.

Wittman, Patricia. **Scrabble Creek.** Macmillan, 1993.

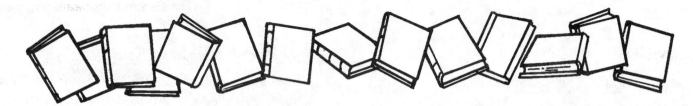

The Berenstain Bears and the Messy Room

Written and Illustrated by Stan and Jan Berenstain

Random House, 1983

Summary

The Berenstain Bears live in a fancy tree house in Bear Country. The house is very neat on the outside. The inside is neat, too, except for the room the cubs share. Their room is "a dust-catching, wall-to-wall, helter-skelter mess." It is untidy because Brother and Sister cannot agree about who should do what job. One day, Mama cannot stand the mess any longer so she starts throwing everything out. The cubs protest, and Papa comes to the rescue with an idea. He will organize the room with specially labeled boxes and pegboards. Soon the room is as clean and neat as the rest of the house. Brother and Sister agree that a clean room is "a lot more fun."

Hints for Reading Aloud

All the Berenstain Bears books give the reader many opportunities to use all sorts of voices. Sister and Brother need to raise their voices when arguing. Mama is angry. After Papa's loud "Quiet!" he should be the voice of reason.

What to Talk About

Ask your child some or all of the following questions:

- Which rooms in your house are usually neat? Which ones are messy? What makes a room messy?
- Do you like your room to be clean or messy?
- Does Mama have a reason to get angry at the cubs?
- Where are your toys stored when you are not playing with them?
- Do you have any toys like the ones in the pictures?
- Are these bears more like animals or people? Why?
- How does Papa act like your dad? How is he different?

Ideas and Activities

- This might be your chance to get some help straightening up your child's room. However, there's no guarantee! Collect boxes and containers for organizing toys and other belongings. Add labels written or drawn by your child.

- Have your child ask relatives how they got along with their brothers and sisters. Compare what they say with how Sister and Brother act in the story.

- Find other books in which the characters are animals who act like people.

- Brother and Sister Bear have to learn to get along. Cooperation is often difficult for young children to understand. Try role-playing some situations that might encourage this. Explain what you are doing. Then pick up a toy and say you want to play with it. Ask your child what to do about this if he or she doesn't want you to play with the toy. Provide several options if he or she doesn't understand.

- Let your child help put away groceries. If the youngster is small, show where a couple of non-breakable items go. Be sure the items you pick can be put away in places that are within your child's reach.

- Try giving your child a chore to do around the house. This can be as simple as picking up shoes and putting them in the closet. Make sure the task is age appropriate and safe for your child to do. The task should be a good learning experience without being frustrating. After the job is completed, you may wish to give your child a small reward such as a sticker.

- The Berenstain Bears are featured in a series of books. The stories often explain or teach lessons. If there is a problem area you need to talk about with your child, you may find other Berenstain Bears books helpful. Children relate easily to these bears.

- There are a number of Berenstain Bears videos available, including **The Berenstain Bears and the Messy Room** (Random House Home Video, 1988).

Related Reading

Berenstain, Stan and Jan. **Bears in the Night.** Random House, 1971.

Berenstain, Stan and Jan. **Bears on Wheels.** Random House, 1971.

Berenstain, Stan and Jan. **The Berenstain Bears in the Dark.** Random House, 1982.

Sharmat, Marjorie M. **Mooch the Messy.** Harper, 1976.

Ward, Lund. **The Biggest Bear.** Houghton, 1952.

Ziefert, Harriet. **A Clean House for Mole and Mouse.** Viking, 1988.

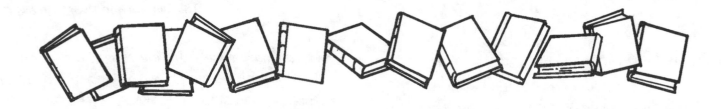

Big Dog, Little Dog

Written and Illustrated by P. D. Eastman

Random House, 1973

Summary

Here's a great story to read at bedtime since it ends with two very tired dogs getting some much needed sleep. Ted and Fred are good friends, but they are very different. Fred is tall while Ted is short. Fred likes to play the flute, eat spinach, drive slowly, and ice skate. Ted prefers the tuba, beets, driving fast, and skiing. After a full day in the snow, the dogs have trouble sleeping because of the sizes of their beds. An observant bird solves their rather simple problem, and both are able to get to sleep.

Hints for Reading Aloud

This is a book of differences and opposites. As you read, emphasize "big-little," "wet-dry," "red-green," and so on. Make the bird sound wise and helpful. When Ted and Fred are discussing their problems, they should sound confused and then very happy as they rush back to bed.

What to Talk About

- Show your child the bird as it appears throughout the book. Discuss how the bird gets to the hotel. Is it the same bird?

- Discuss the differences between Fred and Ted. Talk about how friends can like different things but still like each other. Also discuss what Fred and Ted have in common. Point out that there are just as many similarities as there are differences. For example, both enjoy music, winter sports, vegetables, and painting.

Ideas and Activities

- Have your child compare/contrast one or two friends to him/herself. Throughout life, your child will be asked to compare and contrast what is seen, what is read, what is understood, etc. An older child might be interested in creating a chart with words or pictures.

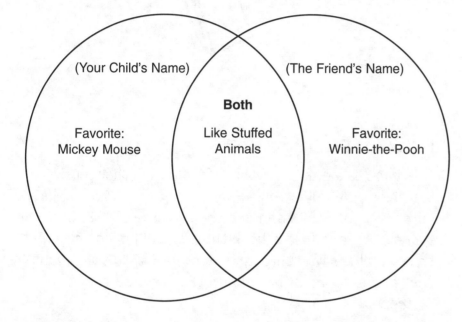

(Your Child's Name)

(The Friend's Name)

Both

Favorite: Mickey Mouse

Like Stuffed Animals

Favorite: Winnie-the-Pooh

- Do some big and little activities. Take some drawing paper and crayons and have your child make little circles. Then have him or her make big circles. Point out the differences. Extend this activity to items you have around the house. For example, show your child a teaspoon and a tablespoon. Ask which is big and which is little. Together find examples of big and little both at home and when you are out.

- Play a game of fast and slow. Choose start and finish lines. This can be as short or long a distance as your child is capable of reaching. Have your child stand at the starting line while you stand at the finish line. Move toward each other. Go slowly enough to let your child reach the opposite side first. Repeat the game, but this time go faster than your child. Ask why the person who goes faster always gets to the opposite side first. Is this always the best way to do things? You may want to tell or read a version of the classic story **The Tortoise and the Hare**. (See the **Related Reading**.)

- Have fun with a tape measure. Get a tape measure and use it to measure various things. Which ones are big and which ones are little? You can also do some measuring with a ruler or a yardstick, but a tape measure can be used to measure around objects. This will help your child begin to understand all types of measurement.

Related Reading

Aesop. **An Aesop Fable: The Tortoise and the Hare.** Holiday, 1984.

Ash, Russell, and Bernard A. Higton, eds. **Aesop's Fables.** Chronicle, 1991.

My First Look at Opposites (from the series **My First Look at**). Random House, 1990.

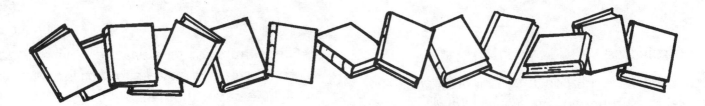

Bread, Bread, Bread

Written by Ann Morris

Photographs by Ken Heyman

Lothrop, Lee and Shepard, 1989

Summary

In this nonfiction book, bread from a variety of cultures is described. The reader is led on a trip around the world seeing all types of different breads that are eaten. The reader not only gets to see breads that are familiar but also many that aren't. Photographs add to the appeal of this book.

Hints for Reading Aloud

This book takes up a rhythm of its own rather quickly. Let the words guide you. As you read this book, make sure that your child can see the pictures of the different types of bread. It is a book that you might not even get to read all the way through before having to talk about the various types of bread and the cultures they represent.

What to Talk About

- Talk about the various types of bread in the book. Ask which ones your child has eaten. Are there any breads shown in the book that your child might like to try?

- Talk about the expression "breaking bread together." What does your child think it means?

Ideas and Activities

- Make bread with your child. A young child can place refrigerator rolls on a cookie sheet. An older child can use a simple recipe or frozen bread dough to make bread. Be sure to serve it with butter and jam. A recipe for Monkey Bread follows.

Monkey Bread

Ingredients: 2 tubes refrigerated buttermilk biscuits, 1/2 cup (125 mL) sugar, 2/3 cup (167 mL) sugar, 1/3 cup (85 mL) of butter or margarine, 1/2 teaspoon (2.5 mL) cinnamon, 1/2 teaspoon (2.5 mL) cinnamon

Directions: Preheat the oven to 350 degrees Farenheit (180 degrees Celsius). Pour 2/3 cup sugar and 1/2 teaspoon cinnamon in a paper bag or cup. Mix. Open each tube of biscuits and cut each biscuit into four parts. Shake the pieces in the bag with the sugar/cinnamon mixture. Place the coated pieces evenly in two greased bread pans. Put 1/2 cup sugar, 1/2 cup butter or margarine, and 1/2 teaspoon cinnamon in a small pot and bring it to a boil, stirring constantly. Boil for one minute. Pour half of the mixture evenly over each pan of biscuits. Bake for 1/2 hour.

- Take your child to a bakery. Find out about some of the breads that are baked there. Are some of them the same as those found in the book? Be adventurous and try a type of bread you wouldn't normally eat. With your child check your pantry. What types of breads do you have?

- Experiment with making some of your favorite sandwiches on breads that you normally wouldn't use. For instance, if your child eats peanut butter and jelly on white bread, try putting it on crackers. Then do a taste comparison. Which does your child like better?

- The Index in **Bread, Bread, Bread** lets you know where all the breads featured in the book are from. Get a world map and point out some of these places to your child.

Related Reading

Coyle, Rena. **My First Baking Book.** Workman, 1988.

Draznin, Sharon. **Simple Cooking Fun.** Teacher Created Materials, 1997.

Drew, Helen. **My First Baking Book.** Knopf, 1991.

Turner, Dorothy. **Bread** (from the series **Foods We Eat**). Carolrhoda, 1989.

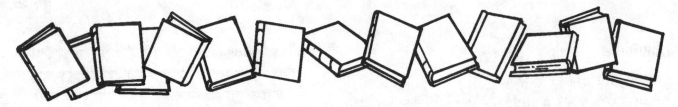

Brown Bear, Brown Bear

Written by Bill Martin, Jr.

Illustrated by Eric Carle

Henry Holt and Company, 1967, 1983

Summary

This primary book asks many animals what they see. Each familiar animal is a different color. At the end of the book are a mother and a group of children who recount what they have seen in the book.

Hints for Reading Aloud

The book is written in a meter or rhythm. You can try emphasizing this the first time you read it. The second time, emphasize the color of the animals. The third time, emphasize the words "you" and "me." If your child is at least two, she or he may be ready to join you in one of the activities described on the next page.

What to Talk About

- Your child can make the sound of each animal when it appears in the book. Ask what each animal would feel like. Which color does your child like most? Which animal would make the best pet? After reading the book a number of times, ask, "Which animal does the (type of animal) see?" before you turn each page. If your child omits the color, ask "What color is the (type of animal)?" Your child might think it's fun to tell you if each animal is larger or smaller than the one before.

- Examine the picture of the children. Discuss the different cultures and variety of clothing. An older child might be able to relate this page to the fact that dogs or cats come in many sizes and colors. You might talk about what humans can do that animals cannot. Don't miss the opportunity to also point out that animals can do certain tasks better than humans.

Ideas and Activities

• Young children enjoy reading books that repeat the same phrases over and over. Just as adults like to hear favorite songs, a child finds nursery rhymes and books like this one entertaining. Your librarian can help you find many other primary "repeating" books. Before you know it, your two- or three-year-old will have partially memorized a whole shelfful of books.

• Make a book to tell your own version of **Brown Bear, Brown Bear.** On each page write down something you see and have your child illustrate it with a bright color. Read your book together. See the Appendix (pages 150–152) for ways to make books with your child.

• Ask your child to help identify the colors. As you read each page, point to the color and see if your child recognizes it. Chances are your youngster will become very accomplished at this the more you read.

• Play a variation of the game "I Spy" called "What Do I See?" Give your child clues about something you see in the room where you are sitting together. Say, "I see something (fill in the appropriate color). What do I see?"

• Ask your child which animal she or he likes the most and look for ways to learn more about it. If it's one of the farm or zoo animals, go to a place where you can watch it. If it is a pet, go to a pet store and talk about the different kinds. If it is an animal you have at home, compare and contrast it to the one in this story.

Related Reading

De Brunhoff, Laurent. **Babar's Book of Colors.** Random, 1984.

McCue, Dick. **Kitty's Colors.** Simon and Schuster, 1983.

Prelutsky, Jack. **Zoo Doings: Animal Poems.** Greenwillow, 1983.

Yenawine, Phillip. **Colors.** Museum of Modern Art, 1991.

Caps for Sale:
A Tale of a Peddler, Some Monkeys, and Their Monkey Business

Told and Illustrated by Esphyr Slobodkina

Young Scott Books, 1940, 1968

Summary

The peddler in this story sells caps for fifty cents. He peddles his wares by stacking them on his head by color: gray, brown, blue, and red. He himself wears a checked cap. One day, he takes a very long nap and awakens to feel somewhat lightheaded. He discovers all of his caps are gone. Looking up, he sees a tree filled with monkeys. Each monkey is wearing one of his caps! This peddler is a clever fellow and gets the pesky monkeys to return his caps in a most amusing way.

Hints for Reading Aloud

The peddler is the only character who speaks. When he calls out "Caps! Caps for sale!" make sure to speak loudly. You may wish to cup your hands around your mouth as someone hawking wares might do. Slow down the pace as the peddler decides to nap. As you read about looking for the caps, shade your eyes with your hands and look around. Pause and let your child guess what the peddler sees. Let your voice show great surprise when the peddler discovers the monkeys wearing the caps. Progressively show anger in your voice as the peddler tries to get back his caps. End the story with some sign of satisfaction when the caps are returned.

What to Talk About

- Ask your child to predict what will happen when the peddler falls asleep.

- The caps cost fifty cents. How much do you think the same type of cap might cost today?

- What does a peddler do? Do we have peddlers or some equivalent today?

- There's an old expression "Monkey see, monkey do." What do you think it means? How does it apply to this story?

- Ask your child to name the various colors of the caps. Why does the peddler wear the checked cap while all the solid colored caps are for sale?

- Talk about the peddler's reasons for getting angry at the monkeys. Ask what makes your child angry and what he or she does about it.

Ideas and Activities

- Recite the fingerplay "Ten Little Monkeys." Do this with the hand movements. Adjust the numbers since ten may be too many to start with.

    Ten little monkeys jumping on the bed, (Show 10 fingers; move hands back and forth.)

    One fell down and bumped his head, (Hold up one finger and shake it; at "bumped" place hand on forehead.)

    Mama called the doctor and the doctor said, (Make a fist with one hand and hold it next to your cheek like you are holding a telephone receiver.)

    "No more monkeys, jumping on the bed." (Hold up one finger and move it across your body as if it's a windshield wiper.)

    Nine little monkeys... (Repeat all motions for each stanza, reducing the number of fingers being held up by one until there aren't any monkeys left.)

- In the story, a cap costs fifty cents. Ask an older child to help you figure out the cost of two caps. Together determine the value of all the peddler's caps.

- Collect as many caps as you can. Compare/contrast caps sold today with those sold by the peddler. Remember this book was first published in 1940.

- Try stacking the caps on your child's head. How many can she or he balance while walking around?

- Let your child make patterns with the hats. These can be stacked one on top of the other or placed on a flat surface. Once the pattern is done, review it together. Then mix up the hats and see if your child can repeat the pattern.

- Try a game of "Monkey See, Monkey Do." Begin by imitating what the peddler does to the monkeys. Then try some of your own ideas such as turning around and jumping on one foot. Take turns being the monkey.

Related Reading

Blos, Joan W. **Martin's Hat.** Morrow, 1984.

McAllister, Angela. **Matepo.** Dial, 1991.

Rey, H. A. **Cecily G. and the Nine Monkeys.** Houghton, 1974.

Rey, H. A. **Curious George.** Houghton Mifflin, 1941, 1969.

Rey, H. A. **Curious George Rides a Bike.** Houghton, 1952.

Schubert, Dieter. **Where's My Monkey?** Puffin, 1992.

Van Allsburg, Chris. **The Wretched Stone.** Houghton, 1992.

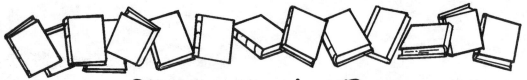

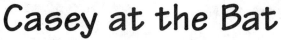

Casey at the Bat

Written by Ernest Lawrence Thayer

Illustrated by Patricia Polacco

Putnam, 1988

Summary

This is an illustrated edition of the famous turn-of-the-century poem. Patricia Polacco has added additional text to bring the poem into modern times. Casey is now a Little Leaguer who arrogantly feels he doesn't have to think much about the big game since, as he says, "Hey, I'm the best." Casey gets his comeuppance with a surprise ending that should delight children who enjoy "America's pastime."

Hints for Reading Aloud

This may be your child's introduction to a long poem. Don't be frustrated if he or she doesn't want to listen to the whole poem every time you read the book. Read the parts your child wants to hear. If your youngster likes the sound of the rhyming couplets—each two lines rhyme—read aloud the poem again and again.

Stress Casey's arrogant dialogue at the beginning so the meaning of the poem is clear. Point out that Casey's sister reminds him of their dad's words so the surprise ending is an enjoyable joke. Don't worry about explaining all the terms in the poem. If your child willingly sits through your reading, the poem's meaning is clear enough. A reader or listener does not have to grasp every word to understand what is occurring. We all understand literature on our own terms, depending on our backgrounds. If you see it through your child's eyes, you'll gain a new perspective.

What to Talk About

- Why does Casey have a bad day at the plate? Does it have anything to do with his behavior before the game? What does his sister mean when she echoes their father's words, "Don't count your hits before they're pitched"? Introduce the well-known expression, "Don't count your chickens before they're hatched."

- Find out whether your child thinks the illustrations go with the poem. How might they be drawn differently?

- Talk about the lesson that Casey learns from this experience. Also, how does his dad put the game into proper perspective at the end?

- What position does your child think Casey plays? Ask him or her for reasons.

Ideas and Activities

- Find an older illustrated version of the poem. How is it different from this one?

- If your child seems interested in the history of baseball, find a photographic history book at the library. Compare past uniforms and stadiums with the modern-day versions.

- Take your child "out to the ball game." Even if there is a major league team in your area, check out a minor league or college game. Here you'll sit close to the action, and your child will be able to see every play.

- Play ball with your child. This can be a game of catch in the yard. A young child can use a plastic bat and ball. Here is a homemade version to play in the house. The bat is a paper towel or wrapping paper tube. The ball is made from wadded up newspaper covered several times with masking tape. If you have a young slugger, you may need to play this outside!

- Check out the sports page of your local newspaper together. Let your child see what is happening in the world of sports. Look at pictures of various athletes. Talk to your child about the different sports that are played.

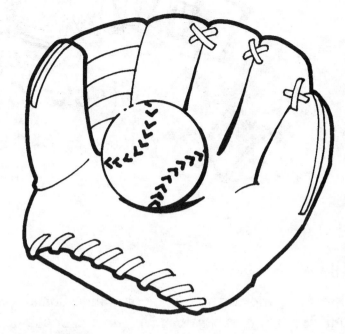

Related Reading

Broeckel, Ray. **Baseball.** Childrens Press, 1982.

Giff, Patricia Reilly. **Ronald Morgan Goes to Bat.** Viking, 1988.

Isadora, Rachel. **Max.** Macmillan, 1976.

Kalb, Jonah. **The Easy Baseball Book.** Houghton, 1976.

McConnachie, Brian. **Elmer and the Chicken vs. the Big League.** Crown, 1992.

Rosenblum, Richard. **Brooklyn Dodger Days.** Macmillan, 1991.

Spohn, David. **Home Field.** Lothrop, 1993.

Stadler, John. **Hooray for the Snail!** HarperCollins, 1984.

Teague, Mark. **The Field Beyond the Outfield.** Scholastic, 1992.

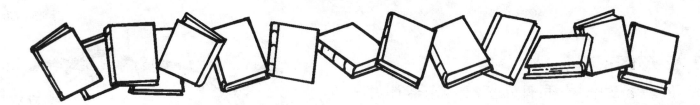

Chicka Chicka Boom Boom

Written by Bill Martin, Jr., and John Archambault

Illustrated by Lois Ehlert

Simon and Schuster, 1989

Summary

An alphabet book with a sense of humor, **Chicka Chicka Boom Boom** has letters climbing up a coconut tree and falling down on top of each other. When the moon comes out, the letters are running up the tree again. The jaunty rhymes and use of nonsense words make this an alphabet book that can be read over and over again.

Hints for Reading Aloud

This is a book that employs nonsense words that help with the rhyme. Read them with a light heart. As each letter talks or is described, read it how it might sound. For example, the letter G should be "all out of breath." Let your child say the letters of the alphabet as you get to each one in the story.

What to Talk About

Ask your child some or all of the following questions:

- What makes this book fun?
- Can letters really climb up a tree?
- What do words like "wiggle-jiggle" or "chicka chicka boom boom" mean?
- How is this book different from other alphabet books? (If you have not read other alphabet books, do so before asking this question.)

Ideas and Activities

- Choose a letter and give a sentence with words that begin with that letter. Pick a subject for the sentence to make it easier. For example, if the subject is food and the letter is L, you might say: Lucy licked lemon frosting off the lemon cake.

- Sing the "Alphabet Song" with your child. There are many recordings of this traditional song. Your child may already know this classic and can sing it for you!

- Look at the letters in the book. They are bright bold colors. With younger children, point out the letters on the inside front and back covers and say their names. If you are working on color recognition, say the color too. "The D in the book is bright pink." For older children, name a word that begins with that letter.

- The letters play in the coconut tree. Find pictures of coconut trees and share them with your child. Where do they grow? Find those places on a map or globe.

- Find a coconut in the produce section of the grocery store. Show it to your child. You may want to purchase it. Ask your child for ideas on how to open it.

- When the full moon comes out, the letters start up again. What is a full moon? Investigate the phases of the moon. Then go outside at night to see them.

- Work together to make your own alphabet book. Collect pictures or small objects that represent a letter and glue them into a page with the letter written on it. See pages 150–152 about making books with children.

- Eat alphabet soup with your child, and have her or him name letters in the soup.

- Your child may enjoy using the following computer software:

  Curious George: ABC Adventure by Houghton Mifflin Interactive. CD-ROM for MAC and PC. Available from Educorp, 7434 Trade Street, San Diego, CA 92121-2410. 1-800-843-9497.

  Chicka Chicka Boom Boom by Kudos. CD-ROM for MAC and WIN. Available from Davidson & Associates, P.O. Box 2961, Torrance, CA 90503. 1-800-545-7677.

Related Reading

Gag, Wanda. **The ABC Bunny**. Putnam, 1933.

Geringer, Laura. **The Cow Is Mooing Anyhow: A Scrambled Alphabet Book to Be Read at Breakfast**. Harper, 1991.

Udry, Janet May. **A Tree Is Nice**. Harper, 1957.

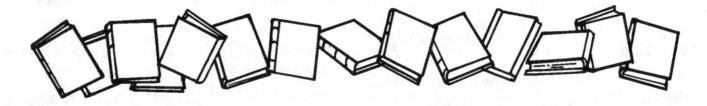

Chicken Little

 Retold and Illustrated by Steven Kellogg

Mulberry Books, 1985

Summary

In this version of the famous folk tale, the villain, Foxy Loxy, plays the central role. He watches the entire progression of events from the very first moment when the acorn hits Chicken Little on the head and she screams, "The sky is falling." He imagines how his huge feast will appear and considers even freezing a few birds for subsequent meals. He makes his move by masquerading as a police officer investigating the falling sky. Gathering all the birds in the police wagon, he heads for his kitchen. However, Sergeant Hippo Hefty in his sky patrol helicopter saves the day. Foxy Loxy is sentenced to prison "on a diet of green-bean gruel and weed juice." Chicken Little lives a long life and continues to tell her famous story until her own grandchildren can listen to the great adventure.

Hints for Reading Aloud

Foxy Loxy should sound menacing but don't disguise his humorous comments. Think of him as one of those villains in an old-time serial who wears a black cape and ties unsuspecting heroines to railroad tracks and says, "Curses, foiled again!" Chicken Little and her friends should be appropriately hysterical as anyone would be if he or she thought the sky was falling.

What to Talk About

- Ask your child if the animals have a reason to be so scared. Remember a small child might think the sky could actually fall. Reassure him or her that this cannot happen. Emphasize Chicken Little's mistake of thinking that the acorn is part of the sky. Point out how the other animals don't ask any questions but just assume that Chicken Little's explanation is correct.

Ideas and Activities

- Find another version of this tale at the library and compare them. Point out how Foxy Loxy plays a larger part in this retelling. Which does your child enjoy more? What makes the Kellogg version funny? What makes this version more modern? Answers include the car and helicopter.

- With your child, make up some rhyming names for other animals such as Kitty Litty, Doggie Woggy, and Sheepy Leepy.

- Chicken Little is called poultry and fowl in the book. Explain that these are group names for birds which can be eaten. See if your child can add another bird to the poultry list. Say "Thanksgiving" as a hint.

- Sergeant Hippo Hefty gives parents a good opportunity to discuss how the police help people. Make sure your child knows how to ask police officers for help.

- Chicken Little planted an acorn and watched it grow. Visit a local nursery and find a small hardy tree that will grow quickly in your area. Your child will enjoy watering it and watching it grow. If you cannot plant a tree, get a window box or other indoor planter and have your child grow some plant or flower seeds.

- Goosey Lucy's little boy is "Gosling Gilbert." Gilbert got his name because a baby goose is a gosling. Ask for names of other baby animals. The chart below contains names of animals and their babies. Can you add to it?

Adult	Baby
cat	kitten
duck	duckling
rooster, hen	chick
vixen, fox	pup, kit
kangaroo	joey
nanny goat, billy goat	kid
cow, bull	calf
ewe, sheep	lamb
goose, gander	gosling

Related Reading

Auch, Mary. **The Easter Egg Farm.** Holiday, 1992.

Carle, Eric. **Roosters Off to See the World.** Picture Book, 1991.

Cazet, Denys. **Lucky Me.** Macmillan, 1983.

Cole, Sheila. **The Hen That Crowed.** Lothrop, 1993.

Czernecki, Stefan, and Timothy Rhodes. **Nina's Treasures.** Hyperion, 1990.

O'Connor, Jane, and Robert O'Connor. **Super Cluck.** Harper, 1991.

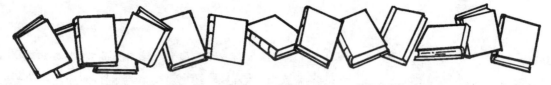

A Child's Garden of Verses

Written by Robert Louis Stevenson

Chronicle Books, 1989

Summary

The classic collection of poems for children of all ages is a delightful trip back in time. This particular edition, conceived and collected by Cooper Edens, features Robert Louis Stevenson's appealing poems as well as illustrations from the late 19th and early 20th centuries.

The poems tell about the child's pastimes in less frenetic times. "Armies in the Fire" tells what a child sees while watching the flames in a fireplace. "Picture-Books in Winter" sings the praises of how a child can enjoy reading in winter. "The Swing" is a poem about the joy of swinging. A child who has been ill will feel empathy for the child in "The Land of Counterpane." "The Flowers" names flowers most people don't know. This book includes more than 50 timeless poems.

Hints for Reading Aloud

These poems, like all poetry, are meant to be read aloud. They are rhythmic and soothing and make for good reading when your child needs a bedtime story and you need to relax. Choose a poem that appeals to you and follow the punctuation. If there is a comma or semicolon, pause. If there is a period, come to a full stop. If there is no punctuation at the end of a line, do not stop or slow down. For a question mark, ask a question with your voice, and for an exclamation point, show excitement.

What to Talk About

- Explain that poetry is a form of writing that sometimes rhymes, uses colorful language, and tells stories in a shortened way. Nursery rhymes are a type of poetry.

- Each poem will evoke various questions you can ask your child. Read the poem first to decide what to talk about specifically. However, there are some general areas you may wish to discuss. In many of the poems, the language will seem old-fashioned because Robert Louis Stevenson lived from 1850–1894. Talk about some of the words and what they mean. This is a great opportunity to work on using context to understand vocabulary. For instance, the word nurse is used repeatedly. What is a nurse? It's comparable to a nanny. How do the poems make you feel? What do you know about the author's feelings from each poem?

Ideas and Activities

Note: Activities for specific poems are given here. Don't let that keep you from reading other poems or doing any type of activity that you feel will work with this book. Many of the activities given can be altered slightly to fit other poems.

- "The Land of Storybooks"—Read this poem and then ask your child what is going on. After determining that the child in the poem is acting out what happens in a story, find a poem or book you both like and act it out!

- "The Swing"—Take your child to a swing, whether in your backyard, the school playground, or the park. Read the poem while swinging gently back and forth. Compare with your child how she or he felt and how the author felt about swinging.

- "Rain"—Help your child memorize this poem or a shorter one in the book. Recite it for someone. Doing this takes practice and determination.

- "Marching Song"—Have a parade with several other children. Make banners and funny hats to wear as described in the poem. Play some marching music, use pot lids as cymbals, and bang pots with wooden spoons for drums. March around the block in "double-quick time."

- "My Shadow"—Do some shadow play. You can do this on a bright sunny day or use lights and do it inside. A slide projector with no slides and just a bulb shining on a screen makes great shadows. You might want to make shadow shapes like some of the ones shown. (butterfly—both hands spread with thumbs overlapped; swan—arm bent at elbow and at wrist, fingers cupped and down)

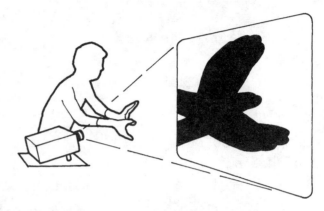

Related Reading

Note: There are several illustrated versions of these poems. The poetry will remain the same, but the art will be different.

Moore, Lillian, ed. **Sunflakes: Poems for Children.** Houghton, 1992.

Prelutsky, Jack. The Random House **Book of Poetry for Children.** Random House, 1983.

Stevenson, Robert Louis. **Block City.** Dutton, 1988.

Stevenson, Robert Louis. **My Shadow.** Putnam, 1990.

Whipple, Laura. **Eric Carle's Dragons and Other Creatures that Never Were.** Putnam, 1991.

Wilson, Sarah. **June Is a Tune That Jumps on a Stair.** Simon and Schuster, 1992.

Zolotow, Charlotte. **Snippets: A Gathering of Poems, Pictures, and Possibilities.** Harper, 1993.

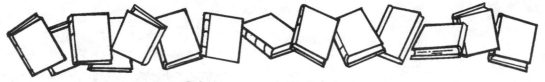

Cleversticks

Written by Bernard Ashley

Illustrated by Derek Brazell

Crown, 1991

Summary

Ling Sung begins school on Monday, but by Wednesday he has had enough. He just can't do things, like tie his shoes or do up his coat, that the other children can do. His frustration grows as each child can accomplish what he cannot until he inadvertently turns paintbrushes into chopsticks and uses them to pick up a piece of cookie. When everyone claps and Ling Sung shows his classmates how to do this, he begins to enjoy school. He finally learns how to do all the things he couldn't do before.

Hints for Reading Aloud

In the beginning of the book, Ling Sung is very frustrated. Express frustration when you read the narrative about Ling Sung trying to do the various tasks. When Ms. Smith claps at his accomplishments, clap for him. Show happiness in your voice as you read her part and that of Ms. Dhanjal. Take on children's voices as each child explains to Ling Sung how to get the job done. Let his father's voice reflect the pride in his child when he calls Ling Sung "Cleversticks."

What to Talk About

- If you have a youngster in preschool or about to start school, talk about what kinds of things he or she might want to learn. Are some of the things that Ling Sung's friends can do some of the things your child wants to learn to accomplish?

- Talk about how difficult it is to learn something new, from tying your shoe to riding a two-wheeler to driving a car. Talk about the importance of determination and practice so that a skill can be learned and then mastered.

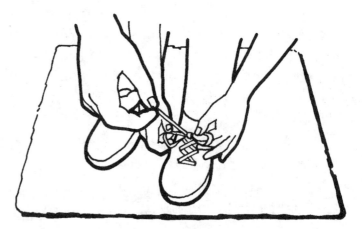

Ideas and Activities

- Together practice using chopsticks. Many Asian restaurants will give you a pair to take home and use. You can also find them on the foreign food aisles in many supermarkets. If you cannot locate real chopsticks, use a pair of unsharpened pencils. Use the directions provided below to learn how to use chopsticks.

1. Place one chopstick in your hand, laying the stick between your thumb and index finger. The chopstick should stay still so don't let it move.

2. Use your thumb, index finger, and two middle fingers to hold the second chopstick. This chopstick will move to pick up the food.

3. Keep the bottom points of the chopsticks even. Move the second chopstick to "pinch" the food against the first chopstick. Pick up the food and eat it.

- In the story, Manjit knew how to write her name. Practice this with your child. Write your child's name in large letters and have him or her trace it.

- Try painting on an easel. It is a different experience from painting on a table. If you can't provide an easel, try an alternative that allows your child to stand and paint. You can tape the paper to a fence outside or use magnets or tape to attach it to the refrigerator door. If you paint inside, place newspaper on the floor to keep it clean. Make sure you provide a few colors and paintbrushes of various sizes. Don't forget to use aprons or smocks since painting can be messy.

- Tying shoes is a difficult task for some children. Let your child practice. Make a shoe to practice on by taking a paper plate and folding it into thirds. Punch four to six holes up either side. Thread a shoelace through the holes and let your child practice tying the shoe. Also, let your youngster practice tying other shoes.

- Putting on jackets can also be tough for children. Practice the way Sharon showed Ling Sung. Have your child begin at the top or the bottom of the jacket.

- Ling Sung made a clown face. What is a clown face? Decide with your child what clown faces look like. Then practice making them in a mirror.

Related Reading (Books About School)

Cazet, Denys. **Never Spit on Your Shoes.** Orchard Books, 1990.

Cohen, Miriam. **First Grade Takes a Test.** Dell, 1983.

Hennessy, B. G. **School Days.** Viking, 1990.

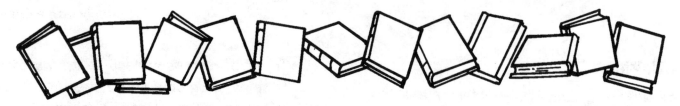

Cloudy with a Chance of Meatballs

Written by Judi Barrett

Illustrated by Ron Barrett

Aladdin, 1978

Summary

In this modern day tall tale, the reader visits the land of Chewandswallow where the food comes from the sky. And what amazing food descends on the people! There are pancakes; frankfurters, already in rolls; sunnyside-up eggs; and all sorts of wonderful foods. The food was the best weather there was until "the weather took a turn for the worse." Suddenly the food which had been friendly and varied switched to a whole day of broccoli or pea-soup fog. Although no one went hungry, Chewandswallow was not a place the people wanted to live so they left in the most unusual rafts.

Hints for Reading Aloud

This book lends itself to a fun-filled reading. Begin the story as if nothing out of the ordinary is happening. However, when you get to the page with the newspaper, make sure to read the headlines since they help to explain the story. As the story progresses, show some worry in your voice. It is fun to add expressions like "icky" or "yuck" as you finish reading about some of the foods the people ate all day.

This book may seem a little long for young children so you may need to break it into two parts. The natural break comes just before the newspaper page and the change in the weather.

What to Talk About

- This is a tall tale. Talk about how a tall tale takes some elements of truth and exaggerates them. How does this story do that?

- What makes this story so amusing? What are the funniest parts of it?

- The food for the townspeople is preselected. Would you and your child want all your food chosen for you?

- How would you feel if you had to eat nothing but pea soup or cream cheese and jelly sandwiches all day? If you got to choose only one food to eat for an entire day, what would it be?

Ideas and Activities

- Spend time looking at the rich illustrations. Together find some of the "extras" provided in the pictures. For instance, what are the street names on the page where the cream cheese and jelly sandwiches are eaten? (Belly Boulevard and Meat Street) Why would these add richness to the story?

- Grandpa starts the story by making pancakes, and later in the story a pancake falls on the school. Make some pancakes with your child. This can be as easy as using a pancake mix where you simply add water, or you may want to follow the simple recipe below.

Buttermilk Pancake Recipe

Ingredients: 2 cups (500 mL) buttermilk, 2 eggs, 1/8 teaspoon (0.5 mL) salt, 1 1/2 teaspoons (7.5 mL) baking powder, 1 teaspoon (5 mL) baking soda, 1 3/4 cups (440 mL) flour

Directions: Mix the ingredients in a bowl. Use a ladle to drop some mixture onto a hot, greased griddle or frying pan. Flip the pancake when there are bubbles all over the wet side. Cook it until it is brown. Serve with butter and syrup.

- The Sanitation Department tried to keep everything clean in Chewandswallow. Find out how your community accomplishes this task.

- The rafts and temporary houses were built from stale bread and peanut butter. Let your child use stale bread and peanut butter to build some kind of structure. Remind him or her not to eat this structure when it's finished.

- Pay attention to the weather report for the next few days. Does it ever have anything to do with the food you eat?

- Many foods are mentioned in this story. Try some new ones with your child.

- Read some other tall tales with your child. Some of them include characters such as Pecos Bill and Slew Foot Sue.

- If your child enjoys this story, he or she might like the video **James and the Giant Peach** (Walt Disney Home Video).

Related Reading

Carle, Eric. **Pancakes, Pancakes!** Scholastic, 1990.

Chalmers, Audrey. **Hundreds and Hundreds of Pancakes.** Viking, 1942.

dePaola, Tomie. **Pancakes for Breakfast.** Scholastic, 1991.

Osborne, Mary Pope. **American Tall Tales.** Knopf, 1991.

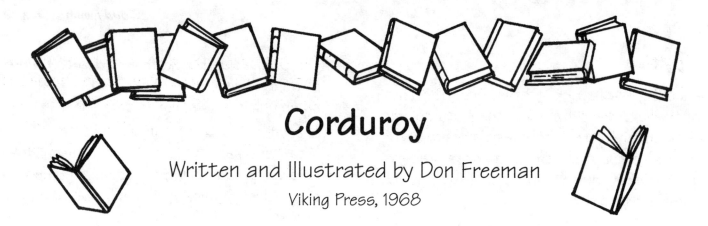

Corduroy

Written and Illustrated by Don Freeman

Viking Press, 1968

Summary

Corduroy is a stuffed bear who lives in the toy section of a department store. He waits patiently for someone to take him home, but no one wants him. One day a young girl (Lisa) wants Corduroy, but her mother says the bear looks old and is missing a button on his overalls. That night, Corduroy searches the store for his lost button. He takes a ride on the escalator and hops on a mattress. A night watchman takes him back to the toy section. The next day Lisa returns and buys the bear. She takes Corduroy to her fourth-floor apartment. Corduroy looks around Lisa's room and realizes it is much better than the store because it is a home. As Lisa sews a button on Corduroy's overalls, they both realize how nice it is to have a friend.

Hints for Reading Aloud

Corduroy continually repeats the line "I guess I've always wanted to . . ." Emphasize this so the last lines of the book make the impression that the author wanted. The night watchman should sound appropriately confused. Lisa should sound kind and extremely happy about having Corduroy for her very own.

What to Talk About

Ask your child some or all of the following questions:

- Which toys in the toy section of the department store would you like to have? (You may wish to ask younger siblings which toys they would like to have, too.)
- Were you surprised when Corduroy started talking and walking?
- Have you been in a department store that carries furniture? If so, what did you see there?
- What are the buttons on a mattress for? How are they different from the buttons on your clothes?
- Why is Lisa so happy about getting Corduroy?
- Which of your toys is the most valuable to you? Why?
- Lisa felt that Corduroy was her friend. Do you consider any of your toys to be your friends? Why or why not?
- How is your room like Lisa's? How is it different?

Ideas and Activities

- Visit a toy store and see if there are any stuffed animals that look like Corduroy.

- Explore a department store. Check out the bedding department and let your child try a few beds. Ride the escalator. Before going to the department store, review escalator safety with your child.

- An older child may enjoy learning how to sew on a button. Get a piece of fabric and some rather large buttons. Help your child thread a large darning needle. Knot the thread, and let your youngster try to sew on the button. It will be much trickier than she or he thinks.

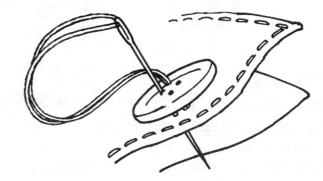

- Many overalls are made out of corduroy fabric. This might be how Corduroy the bear got his name. Find something made out of corduroy fabric and let your child touch it. How does it feel?

- Your child might enjoy watching the movie version of **Corduroy** (Wood Knapp Video, 1993). Also available on tape is **A Pocket for Corduroy**.

Related Reading

Freeman, Don. **Beady Bear.** Puffin, 1954.

Freeman, Don. **Bearymore.** Viking, 1976.

Freeman, Don. **A Pocket for Corduroy.** Viking, 1978.

Glen, Maggie. **Ruby.** Putnam, 1991.

Graham, Amanda. **Who Wants Arthur?** Stevens, 1987.

Hissey, Jane. **Old Bear.** Putnam, 1991.

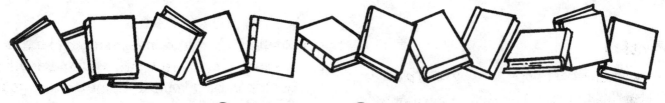

Curious George

Written and Illustrated by H. A. Rey

Houghton Mifflin, 1941, 1969

Summary

In the first of the **Curious George** books, the man with the yellow hat befriends George, a curious little monkey, in Africa. The man decides to bring George to the United States with him. George's adventures begin as he tries on the yellow hat. His escapades on the big ship are almost his last. Further adventures have George calling the fire station in error, being put in prison, and floating into the sky with a group of balloons. Through it all, this monkey will keep young ones intrigued with his "monkey sense."

Hints for Reading Aloud

Curious George is a book that mostly describes the monkey and his adventures so take advantage of the parts in the story that allow for drama. Most of these are written in capital letters so that you will have no trouble finding them. Make sure that your voice shows some anxiousness as it describes some of George's antics, such as falling overboard. When reading the part about the fireman, you may wish to slightly hurry your voice as the firefighters frantically search for a nonexistent fire.

What to Talk About

Ask your child some or all of the following questions:

- George is a curious monkey. What is curiosity? How does George's curiosity get him into trouble?
- Would you describe George as naughty? Why or why not?
- What are some things that George does that are amusing?
- Why was it wrong for George to call the fire department, even by mistake?
- Did it make sense to put a monkey in prison?
- What are some of the animal characteristics that George has? What are some of the human characteristics the author gives him?
- What events in the story could really happen?

Ideas and Activities

- As the book was written in 1940, some of the pictures in **Curious George** may look out of date to you and your child. Take a look at some of these, such as the telephone or hook and ladder truck. Find modern pictures of them. Let your child describe what is different about them.

- George called the fire station by mistake. Explain that this could be a costly error because it tied up the firefighters' time when there might have been a true emergency. Then tell when it is appropriate to call the fire department. Show your child the correct way to summon help from the fire department.

- Visit a fire station. Make arrangements in advance or find out when your community is holding an open house at a nearby fire station. Compare the trucks and uniforms that are in the story to those of contemporary firefighters.

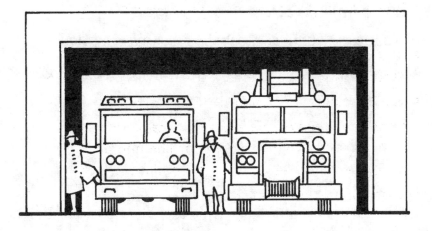

- Monkeys will sometimes imitate behavior as George does when he tries to fly like the seagull. With your child, try imitating each other. For instance, stand on one foot and then have your child try to do the same. After all of his adventures, George gets to live in the zoo. If you live near a zoo, visit it with your child. Spend some time at the primate exhibits where you will see monkeys and other related animals.

- Read **Caps for Sale.** (See pages 32 and 33.) How are the monkeys in that story like George? George is a funny little monkey. Read some other **Curious George** books to find out about some of his other adventures. (See the **Related Reading** for suggestions.) Compare the other **Curious George** stories to this book. Which one do you and your child like best? Why?

- Your child can have more fun with **Curious George** using the following computer software: **Curious George: Early Learning Adventure** or **Curious George: ABC Adventure** by Houghton Mifflin Interactive. CD-ROM for MAC and PC. Available from Educorp, 7434 Trade Street, San Diego, CA 92121-2410. 1-800-843-9497.

Related Reading

Rey, Margaret. **Curious George Flies a Kite.** Houghton, 1973.

Rey, Margaret. **Curious George Rides a Bike.** Houghton, 1952.

Slobodkina, Esphyr. **Caps for Sale.** Young Scott Books, 1940, 1968.

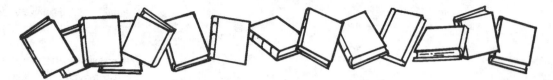

The Day Jimmy's Boa Ate the Wash

Written by Trinka Hakes Noble

Illustrated by Steven Kellogg

Dial, 1980

Summary

Take a rollicking romp as Jimmy and his classmates go on a field trip to a farm. As a mother asks her daughter about the trip, the details of the rather frenetic trip unfold. From falling haystacks to flying chickens to the boa mentioned in the title, the class trip is a lark. Steven Kellogg's delightful illustrations contribute to the hilarity of this story.

Hints for Reading Aloud

This is a story told in dialogue as a mother questions her daughter about the class trip to a farm. As the story is read, take on the voice of a curious mother when asking questions about the trip. Injecting the mother's lines with a certain amount of disbelief will keep the action moving. When the daughter speaks, use a noncommittal tone, as though leaving a boa constrictor on a farm is an everyday occurrence.

What to Talk About

Ask your child some or all of the following questions:

- Show your child the delightful drawings in this book. What is happening in the pictures? Do the illustrations contribute to the story?

- Which incidents in the story seem like they could really happen?

- What makes this book funny?

- Why do you think the girl isn't terribly excited or upset about what happened at the farm?

Ideas and Activities

- Visit a farm. Talk about the animals and what they produce. For example, we get wool from sheep and eggs from chickens. If a farm is not available, try a county fair. If you live on a farm, compare your home with the farm in the story.

- The children go on a field trip to the farm. Most field trips are not quite so chaotic. If your child has not been on any field trips, this would be a good opportunity to talk about them. You can review safety rules such as listening to the teacher/group leader, staying with a buddy, and not wandering away from the group.

- Not all field trips need to be taken with large groups. You may wish to arrange one for your family. Museums, factory tours, and parks you have never visited are relatively inexpensive or free and make enjoyable outings.

- Find out about boa constrictors. How they eat is especially interesting to children. If possible, look at them in a pet store or the reptile house at the zoo.

Otherwise, learn more by reading an encyclopedia or other nonfiction books. How big do boa constrictors get? Investigate this and then, using a roll of shelf or butcher paper, make a life-size drawing of one.

- This story lends itself to determining the difference between real and make-believe. Together decide which incidents could be real and which are make-believe.

- Look at the picture of the pigs eating the students' lunches. What did the children bring to eat? List as many of the foods as you can. Then decide with your child which of those items to pack for your child's field trip lunch.

- First, Jimmy has a pet boa constrictor which he exchanges for a pig. If you have a pet, talk about it. What are the responsibilities of having an animal? Make a list of animals that would make good pets. Does a boa constrictor appear on it?

- Rent the video **The Day Jimmy's Boa Ate the Wash** (Wood Knapp Video, 1994) or **A Day at Old MacDonald's Farm** (Warner Communications, 1985).

Related Reading

Bender, Lionel. **Pythons and Boas.** Watts, 1988.

Bodsworth, Nan. **A Nice Walk in the Jungle.** Viking, 1990.

Noble, Trinka Hakes. **Jimmy's Boa and the Big Splash Birthday Bash.** Dial, 1989.

Simon, Seymour. **Meet the Giant Snakes.** Walker, 1979.

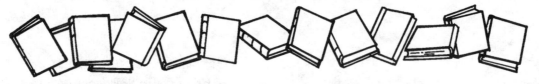

Emma's Christmas

Resung and Illustrated by Irene Trivas

Orchard Books, 1988

Summary

In this delightful retelling of the classic "On the First Day of Christmas," a prince proposes to a farm girl who is reluctant to accept him as a husband. The prince then woos his lady love by sending her all the items mentioned in the song. Each day he repeats the same items so by the twelfth day she has 12 partridges, 22 turtle doves, and so on. It's really enough to make a girl say yes to a prince!

Hints for Reading Aloud

Of course, this story shouldn't be read—it should be sung! Even if you can't sing, do your best at warbling out the tune. The traditional melody is available in many Christmas songbooks or on a Christmas CD, record, or cassette tape. Of course, you should let your child join in. Even very young children will recognize the repetitive language and be able to join in with some of the words.

There are some parts of the story that should be read. You should read these in clear tones, squawking out "EMMA" as the calling birds do and showing the mother's disgust at all the presents.

What to Talk About

- Ask your child what all the things in the story are. Which ones does he or she know and which ones does he or she need to find out about? Explain what the unfamiliar items are and, if possible, show additional pictures of them.

- At the beginning of the book, ask your child to predict what will happen by the end of the story. Will the farm girl say yes to the prince? Was the ending a surprise? If you have a son, ask if he would propose in such a fashion. If you have a daughter, ask if she would enjoy being wooed in such a way. If you have sons and daughters, make this topic a family discussion.

Ideas and Activities

- Sing the traditional version of "On the First Day of Christmas." Encourage your child to join in. Sing other Christmas carols. For younger children, try some simple ones, such as "Deck the Halls," since it will be easy for them to learn "fa la la la la, la la, la la."

- Emma receives many gifts. With your child, try to tally the total. You can do this several different ways, such as all the calling birds or all the French hens or a combination of the two. (The last page tells how many of each gift she receives.)

- Talk about Christmas gifts. Work together to make a gift for someone special. This could be an edible treat, a drawing, or a book that you make. Create a unique Christmas card. Ask your child to go with you when you deliver the present.

- Share other classic Christmas stories such as **The Grinch Who Stole Christmas** by Dr. Seuss (Random, 1957) or **The Night Before Christmas.**

- Have a Christmas cookie party. Let your child invite a few friends and read **Emma's Christmas** to them.

- For young children, this book can easily be used as a counting book. Choose one of the gifts and find it on the pages that list everything. Count how many of those items actually appear on the page. Are some hiding? Make up simple addition or subtraction problems.

- At the end of the story, there is a huge crowd of people, animals, and trees, just to name a few. Talk about how to behave when in a crowd (stay close, hold hands, etc.). When you are in a crowd remind your child about **Emma's Christmas** and stress the importance of staying together.

- Take your child to a Christmas concert. There are many free ones given during the holiday season. Beginning in November, check your local newspaper for performances where you live.

Related Reading

Baird, Anne. **The Christmas Lamb.** Morrow, 1989.

Carrier, Lark. **A Christmas Promise.** Picture Book, 1991.

dePaola, Tomie. **Jingle the Christmas Clown.** Putnam, 1992.

dePaola, Tomie. **Merry Christmas, Strega Nona.** Harcourt, 1986.

Edens, Cooper. **Santa Cows.** Simon & Schuster, 1991.

Gantos, Jack. **Rotten Ralph's Rotten Christmas.** Houghton, 1984.

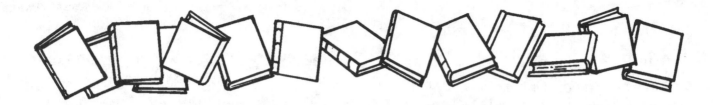

Everett Anderson's Goodbye

Written by Lucille Clifton

Illustrated by Ann Grifalconi

Henry Holt and Company, 1983

Summary

In this poignant story, Everett Anderson goes through the five stages of grief—denial, anger, bargaining, depression, and acceptance—as he copes with the death of his father. The book is divided into five lovely, touching poems that describe Everett's recovery from the loss of someone so dear to him.

Hints for Reading Aloud

Each of the stages of grief are written in poetry form. Carefully follow the punctuation, pausing at the commas and coming to a full stop at the periods. At the end of each poem, stop for a few seconds before beginning the next poem. Have a bit of resolve in your voice when you read Everett's last statement.

What to Talk About

- This book is especially helpful for children if someone in your family has recently passed away. **Everett Anderson's Goodbye** is a story about coming to grips with the death of a father. Talk to your child about what death is in terms with which you are comfortable with.

- The book is dedicated "to my sad friends." Explain who these might be and what makes people sad. Talk about how people feel sad and how they often cry. With your child think of things that you could do that might make someone who is grieving feel better.

- Discuss the emotions expressed by each of the poems in the book. Ask your child to describe times when he or she felt as Everett does.

Ideas and Activities

- This story is really five poems. With your child, write a poem about someone you really care about who is no longer alive.

- Share some positive remembrances of someone you knew who has passed away. These can be in story form, a photograph, or a momento you have that belonged to that person. Invite your child to share some of these memories with you.

- The pictures in this book are particularly appropriate, showing Everett with a tear at the beginning and a smile at the end. Show your child how the words match the expressions in the pictures. Let your child try using just a pencil and a piece of paper to imitate the technique seen in the drawings.

Related Reading

Clifton, Lucille. **The Boy Who Didn't Believe in Spring.** Dutton, 1973.

Clifton, Lucille. **Some of the Days of Everett Anderson.** Henry Holt, 1970.

Cohn, Janice. **I Had a Friend Named Peter: Talking to Children About the Death of a Friend.** Morrow, 1987.

Jukes, Mavis. **I'll See You in My Dreams.** Knopf, 1993.

Lanton, Sandy. **Daddy's Chair.** Kar-Ben, 1991.

Porte, Barbara Ann. **Harry's Mom.** Greenwillow, 1985.

Simon, Norma. **The Saddest Time.** Whitman, 1986.

Viorst, Judith. **The Tenth Good Thing About Barney.** Atheneum, 1971.

Zolotow, Charlotte. **My Grandson Lew.** Harper, 1973.

Everybody Cooks Rice

Written by Norah Dooley

Illustrated by Peter J. Thornton

Carolrhoda Books, 1991

Summary

Carrie's mother asks her to find her younger brother, Anthony so they can eat dinner. Since Anthony often wanders the ethnically diverse neighborhood, Carrie starts off on her search. She first calls on the Darlingtons who are from Barbados. Although Anthony is not there, Carrie stays long enough to sample their dish of rice and black-eyed peas. Carrie circles the street and at each house has a taste of their special rice dish. Carrie finds that although people come from different parts of the world, they all have rice in common. The recipes provided in the back of the book come from Puerto Rico, Vietnam, India, China, Haiti, and Italy, along with the one from Barbados.

Hints for Reading Aloud

Have Carrie sound very disgusted with her brother at the beginning of the story. The author decided not to have dialogue between Carrie and the neighbors. However, your voice should emphasize the different rice dishes. Read these descriptions slowly and answer any questions your child might have. It might be interesting to use a world map to point out the native countries of the neighbors.

What to Talk About

- Invite your child to tell you what is special about each rice dish. Be sure to discuss the illustrations and point out their special qualities.

- Help your child notice that while Carrie didn't want to go at the beginning, she enjoys talking and eating with the people in her neighborhood. Is it surprising that Anthony is home by the time Carrie returns?

- Point out that Carrie is very hungry at the beginning of the story but is full by the time she returns home. Why?

- Talk about the different ways your child has had rice prepared. Talk about the ways your child has eaten rice at home, at a friend's house, and at a restaurant. What are your child's favorite rice dishes?

Ideas and Activities

- This book includes several recipes. Try one or two that your child can help prepare. **Warning:** Escaping steam from a pot of rice can cause serious burns.

- Visit a restaurant that serves rice in a new and special way.

- A relative may have a special rice recipe to cook for your child. Or go to the library and introduce your child to one or two brightly illustrated cookbooks.

- How many grains of rice do you think might be in a cup? Measure out a cup of uncooked rice, and divide it into fourths. Count out how many grains are in one-fourth cup. Then multiply by four to estimate how much would be in a cup.

- Find a book on another type of food eaten almost everywhere on Earth, such as bread. Examine the different types of bread that are available at grocery stores.

- Let your child make a rice picture. Use cardboard, a thick marker, glue, and grains of rice. Make an outline drawing with the marker. Fill in the gaps by spreading a thin layer of glue. Cover the glue with the rice.

- Just in case you need one more rice recipe, here's one for rice pudding.

Rice Pudding

Ingredients: 1 cup (250 mL) uncooked rice, 2 cups (500 mL) water, 1 package vanilla pudding mix (This needs to be the type that is cooked.), 1 $^3/_4$ to 2 cups (440–500 mL) milk (Check the pudding package for an exact amount.), $^1/_2$ cup (125 mL) raisins

Directions: Using 1 cup of uncooked rice and 2 cups of water, follow the rice package directions. Cool the rice. Prepare the cooked pudding as directed on package, using the mix and milk. Cool. Mix the rice pudding together in a large bowl. Add $^1/_2$ cup raisins. Serve.

Related Reading

Friedman, Ina. **How My Parents Learned to Eat.** Houghton Mifflin, 1984.

Morris, Ann. **Bread, Bread, Bread.** Lothrop, Lee and Shepard, 1989.

Morrison, Lynne. **Rice.** Carolrhoda, 1990.

Sproule, Anna. **Food for the World.** Facts on File, 1987.

Thompson, Ruth. **Rice.** Garrett, 1990.

Turner, Dorothy. **Bread.** Carolrhoda Books, 1988.

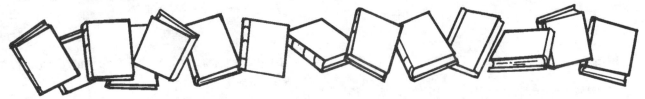

Franklin in the Dark

Written by Paulette Bourgeois

Illustrated by Brenda Clark

Scholastic, 1986

Summary

Franklin is afraid of the dark. But for Franklin the problem is greater than for most because Franklin is a turtle who has to crawl into his shell to go to sleep. Even with his mother's reassurance that there are no monsters or slippery things in his shell, Franklin is frightened. He goes on an adventure and meets other animals who share their fears with him, such as a lion who is afraid of loud noises. He returns home to find that even his mother has great fears. Franklin now understands how to conquer his fears.

Hints for Reading Aloud

Franklin is a turtle with great fear of the dark. However, he is brave enough to find out from other animals some ways to overcome his fears. As you read Franklin's part, make his voice sound a bit wistful so the fear can be overcome. Give Franklin a young voice. Have the other characters sound kindly as they offer to help Franklin by telling about their own fears. Have Mother Turtle sound very frightened when she tells Franklin she thought that he was lost. Let the "hmmmm's" sound full of realization.

What to Talk About

- Franklin has many fears. Talk to your child about his or her fears. What kinds of things does your child find frightening? Talk about ways to overcome these fears.

- All the animals offer to help Franklin. Ask your child to explain why the animals couldn't really do anything for Franklin. What would your child offer to do to help Franklin overcome his fears?

Ideas and Activities

• Franklin was afraid of the dark. His mother used a flashlight, and he used a night-light to help overcome his fear. Let your child play with a flashlight and show how it can help ease the fear of the dark. Many children like to keep flashlights next to their beds to have after dark.

• Find out more about real turtles. In the story, Franklin takes off his shell. Find out what would happen to a real turtle if its shell came off. How do turtles sleep? Look at the pictures of Franklin's shell. It has a mosaic quality. Create a simple mosaic turtle shell pattern with your child. Draw a simple outline of a turtle shell on a piece of cardboard. Cut up differently colored pieces of construction paper into squares of various sizes. Show your child how to glue the squares to fill in the shell.

• What other animals have shells that are their homes? Go into a garden and see if you can find any snails, or check out some crabs at the seashore. Do these animals pull their heads inside their shells?

• Many children are afraid of the dark and going to bed. Read some other books that talk about bedtime fears while giving children different ways to deal with this type of situation.

• Your children may enjoy conquering a fear of monsters by creating some of their own using the following computer software: **Awesome Animated Monster Maker** by Houghton Mifflin Interactive. CD-ROM for MAC and PC. Available from Educorp, 7434 Trade Street, San Diego, CA 92121-2410. 1-800-843-9497.

Related Reading

Alexander, Martha. **I'll Protect You from the Jungle Beasts.** Dial, 1983.

Babbitt, Natalie. **The Something.** Farrar, 1987.

Chevalier, Christa. **Spence and the Sleepytime Monster.** Whitman, 1984.

Cooper, Helen. **The Bear Under the Stairs.** Dial, 1993.

Howe, James. **There's a Monster Under My Bed.** Macmillan, 1986.

Lobby, Ted. **Jessica and the Wolf: A Story for Children Who Have Bad Dreams.** Brunner, 1990.

Waber, Bernard. **Ira Sleeps Over.** Houghton, 1973.

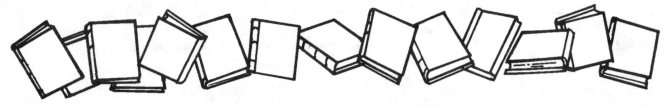

The Gingerbread Boy

Retold and Illustrated by Paul Galdone

Clarion, 1975

Summary

In this classic fairy tale, a little old lady bakes a gingerbread boy. She forgets him in the oven, and when she goes to take him out, he runs away! He is chased by a myriad of people and animals who try to catch him. It is not until the crafty fox offers to take him across the river that the gingerbread boy meets his fate.

Hints for Reading Aloud

This story lends itself to reading aloud due to the repetition of the Gingerbread Boy's lines. When you read his first lines of "Run! Run! Run! Catch me if you can! You can't catch me! I'm the Gingerbread Boy, I am! I am!" you will need to read them tauntingly. Throughout the story, the Gingerbread Boy's lines get longer as a different animal or group chases him. Make him sound more confident with each reading of his rhyme.

When you read the fox's lines, make him sound sincere so your child will really believe the Gingerbread Boy would jump up on the fox's nose. You may want to brush your hands together when you get to "Snip," and then "Snip, Snap." Read the line written in capital letters in a very loud voice and then finish the story with a slightly smug air. In subsequent readings, encourage your child to say the rhyme with you.

What to Talk About

- Your child may be upset that the Gingerbread Boy gets eaten. If so, talk about why that might be upsetting.
- Ask how your child felt when the Gingerbread Boy jumped up, talked, and ran away. Could this really happen?
- Talk about the fox. How did he manage to outsmart everyone else who wanted to eat the Gingerbread Boy?
- What lesson does the story teach about being boastful?

Ideas and Activities

- Make a gingerbread boy or girl with your child. You can make one using cookie cutters and a mix. Let your child help by adding ingredients, stirring the mixture, and cutting the dough. If you do not have a cookie cutter, enlarge the pattern on this page and make a template to place on the dough. Then cut around it. Provide frosting and any other edible goodies to decorate the cookies. You may prefer to buy prepackaged gingerbread boy cookies to decorate. If this is the first time your child has eaten gingerbread, ask if she or he likes it.

- Read other versions of this classic. Some of them are called **The Gingerbread Man.** Compare them. Which does your child like best? Why?

- Make a sewing card in the shape of a gingerbread boy or girl. Enlarge the pattern on this page or use a cookie cutter. Trace it onto heavy brown paper. Cut it out. Then use a hole punch and punch holes at even intervals around the edges. Give your child a long piece of white yarn or shoelaces. If you use yarn, wrap a piece of tape around the end to make it easier for your child to use when sewing. Show how to thread the yarn or shoelaces through the holes to decorate the sewing card. To make a stuffed gingerbread boy, make two copies of the pattern. Place them back to back. Staple or tape them about three-quarters of the way around. Stuff them with crumpled up newspaper or tissue paper. Close the opening.

- Give your child some play dough or clay. Have him or her make gingerbread boys and girls and decorate them. If you use the type of clay that dries, put a hole at the top, and you will have a homemade ornament.

- Sing this gingerbread song to the tune of "A Peanut Sat on a Railroad Track." You can substitute gingerbread girl for boy.

Soft and Gooey

A gingerbread boy is quite a sight,
He's soft, he's brown, he's gooey,
He smiles, he winks, he jumps, he runs,
Quick, gobble him up, he's chewy.

Related Reading

Jarrell, Randall. **The Gingerbread Rabbit.** Macmillan, 1972.

Kimmel, Eric. **The Gingerbread Man.** Holiday, 1992.

Wilburn, Kathy. (Illustrator). **The Gingerbread Boy**. Putnam, 1984.

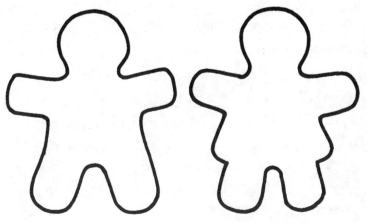

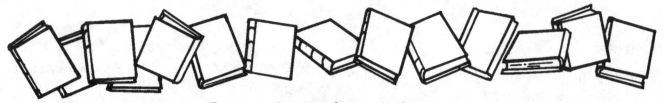

Goodnight Moon

Written by Margaret Wise Brown

Illustrated by Clement Hurd

HarperCollins Children's Books, 1947, 1975

Summary

"In the great green room" every object gets its own special goodnight greeting. All the objects that are bid goodnight are shown as both a part of a large, colored illustration of a bedroom and then individually in black and white.

Hints for Reading Aloud

Goodnight Moon is the classic story for reading at bedtime. Little ones have listened to the story since 1947. This book is usually read at night or before nap time. It lends itself to being read in soft, quiet tones. Allow your voice to follow the rhythm of the lines.

The book has no punctuation so some prereading may be necessary to determine in advance where you want to pause. The best places for this will be at the end of a rhyme. Don't worry about prereading too many times. You will read this book so frequently that you will have it memorized before long!

What to Talk About

Ask your child some or all of the following questions:

- To whom or what do you like to say goodnight?
- Talk about bedtime. What do you like best about going to bed? What do you like least about going to bed?
- What objects shown in the book are like those that you own? Do they look the same? Do you say goodnight to them? Draw comparisons among objects in your child's bedroom and those in the book.

Ideas and Activities

- Bedtime rituals vary for each child and family. Determine what yours are or will be. Depending on your child's age, let him or her be part of the decision-making process. A young child can select which activity is first, such as putting on pajamas or brushing teeth.

- Look through the illustrations in the story. Let your child see how the pictures darken. Ask what is happening. (The sun is going down, and it is getting darker outside.) Show your child the progression of light to dark in the book. Then show what happens in your surroundings. This can be done by looking out the window in the evening. Talk about night and day.

- In **Goodnight Moon** there is a picture of a cow jumping over the moon. This reference is to the nursery rhyme "The Cat and the Fiddle." Show this picture to your child and recite the following nursery rhyme.

    "The Cat and the Fiddle"
    Hey diddle, diddle, the cat and the fiddle,
    The cow jumped over the moon.
    The little dog laughed to see such a sight
    And the dish ran away with the spoon.

Related Reading

Baum, Louis. **I Want to See the Moon.** Viking, 1989.

Blocksma, Mary. **Yoo Hoo, Moon!** Bantam, 1992.

Boyd, Lizi. **Sweet Dreams, Willy.** Viking, 1992.

Brown, Margaret Wise. **A Child's Goodnight Book.** Harper, 1992.

Brown, Margaret Wise. **The Runaway Bunny.** Harper, 1942, 1972.

Brown, Margaret Wise. **The Sleepy Little Lion.** Harper, 1947.

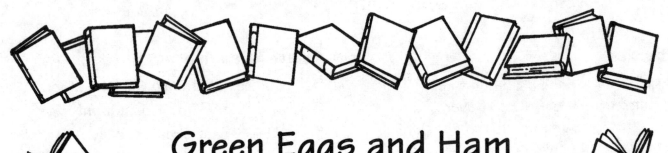

Green Eggs and Ham

Written and Illustrated by Dr. Seuss

Random House, 1960

Summary

Sam-I-Am wants his friend to like green eggs and ham. His friend, just as adamantly, refuses to even try, let alone eat, green eggs and ham. He won't eat them "in a box, on a train, in a car" or any other number of places. Whether it's Sam-I-Am's persuasiveness or just his friend's exasperation at Sam-I-Am's pestering, he tries the green eggs and ham. Much to his surprise, he really likes them!

Hints for Reading Aloud

The book is actually a dialogue between the two characters. Take on two voices, one for Sam-I-Am and one for his friend. When reading the underwater scene, use a wavy voice. On the lists, start low and raise your voice as you go. Pay attention to the exclamation points. Be sure to raise your voice as you get to them.

What to Talk About

Most of us have foods we don't like. Ask your child some or all of the following questions:

- What foods do you dislike?
- What green foods can you think of? Make a list.
- Why do you think Sam-I-Am pestered his friend?
- What do you think green eggs would taste like?

Ideas and Activities

- Practice rhyming words. In subsequent readings, leave out the final word and let your child name a rhyming word—such as tree, bee, see, me, flea.

- Think of some foods that you can dye with green food coloring.

- Have a Green Eggs and Ham Party. Read the story and cook scrambled eggs, adding a bit of green food coloring. Use a favorite recipe or try the one below.

A Green Egg Scramble

Ingredients: 2 eggs, pat of butter, about 1 tablespoon (15 mL) water or milk, a few drops of green food coloring

Directions: Crack the eggs in a bowl and beat them until they're smooth. Add a bit of water or milk to them and a few drops of food coloring. The amount will depend on how green you want your eggs. Place the butter in a frying pan. Melt the butter over a low heat. Then add the eggs. Turn the heat to medium. Stir the eggs until they're set. Serve hot.

- The second character in the story doesn't have a name. Let your child help name this character. You might want to use the same hyphenated and rhyming pattern as Sam-I-Am. List several choices and discuss which is best.

- Visit the Dr. Seuss Web site, Cyber-Seuss. (See **Technology Connections**, page 13.)

- Your child may enjoy the computer software version of this story: **Green Eggs and Ham** by Dr. Seuss; produced by Living Books and Broderbund. CD-ROM for MAC and PC. Available from Educorp, 7434 Trade Street, San Diego, CA 92121-2410. 1-800-843-9497.

- Many Dr. Suess stories are on video, including **Green Eggs and Ham** (Random House Home Video).

Related Reading

Heine, Helme. **The Most Wonderful Egg in the World.** Macmillan, 1983.

Prelutsky, Jack. **The Baby Eggs Are Hatching.** Greenwillow, 1982.

Seuss, Dr. **The Cat in the Hat.** Random, 1957.

Seuss, Dr. **Hop on Pop.** Random, 1963.

Seuss, Dr. **I Can Lick Thirty Tigers Today and Other Stories.** Random, 1969.

Seuss, Dr. **One Fish, Two Fish, Red Fish, Blue Fish.** Random, 1960.

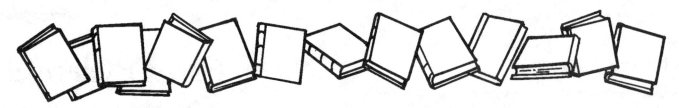

Gregory, the Terrible Eater

Written by Mitchell Sharmat

Illustrated by Jose Aruego and Ariane Dewey

Scholastic, 1980

Summary

Gregory the goat is a most unusual eater, at least for a goat. While his parents despair because he won't eat newspaper, a tool kit, or a broken violin, Gregory is content to eat fish, eggs, and bread. His parents devise a plan to introduce proper goat food to their son while allowing him to enjoy foods not normally associated with "goatful" eating. It is a plan that satisfies everyone all the way around.

Hints for Reading Aloud

Choose different voices for Mother, Father, and Gregory. Throughout the story as you read the dialogue between the parents, let your voice show concern about Gregory's poor eating habits. When Father throws down his paper, put some exasperation into your voice. Read Dr. Ram with the wise authority he exudes. Read distinctly when telling the foods that Gregory eats, especially at the end. This way your child will hear just what type of meals this goat eats. Let Mother finally sound satisfied at the end.

What to Talk About

- At the beginning of the story, Gregory is a picky eater. What does that mean?

- Gregory's mother tells him he shouldn't "eat like a pig." What does this expression mean? How does it apply to Gregory?

- Gregory's parents were really concerned about their son's eating habits. Talk about proper eating habits and how parents show concern for their children. What did Gregory's parents do to help him?

Ideas and Activities

- Goats really are picky eaters. They are browsers who prefer to eat leaves from trees. They are like deer in their eating habits. Do some research about goats to find out more about them.

- Find some goats to pet. These animals are often found on farms and petting zoos. If you have an opportunity, take your child to see some. You may be able to pet and feed them. Just make sure you feed them their proper food!

- Together investigate the food pyramid created by the United States Department of Agriculture (USDA) as a way of presenting our government's latest guidelines for a healthy diet. The categories and proper amounts are shown on the right. With your child, determine which foods fit into each category. Keep a record of what both of you eat for a couple of days. Are you staying within the guidelines?

Related Reading

Carlson, Nancy Savage. **Spooky and the Witch's Goat.** Lothrop, 1989.

Coplans, Peta. **Spaghetti for Suzy.** Houghton, 1993.

Demarest, Chris L. **No Peas for Nellie.** Macmillan, 1988.

Lester, Alison. **Clive Eats Alligators.** Houghton, 1986.

Mahy, Margaret. **The Queen's Goat.** Dial, 1991.

Schoberle, Cecile. **Esmerelda and the Pet Parade.** Simon & Schuster, 1990.

Seuss, Dr. **Green Eggs and Ham.** Random House, 1960.

Food Pyramid

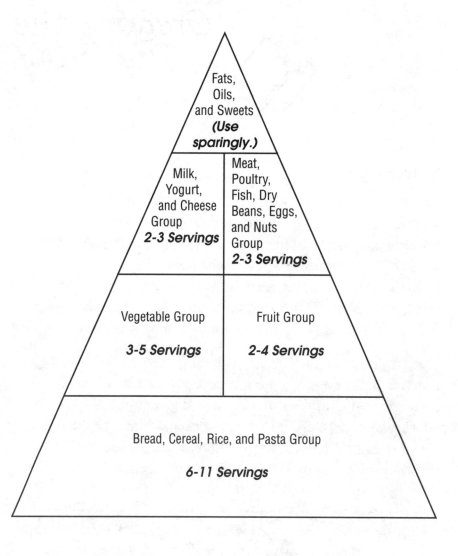

Fats, Oils, and Sweets *(Use sparingly.)*

Milk, Yogurt, and Cheese Group **2-3 Servings**

Meat, Poultry, Fish, Dry Beans, Eggs, and Nuts Group **2-3 Servings**

Vegetable Group **3-5 Servings**

Fruit Group **2-4 Servings**

Bread, Cereal, Rice, and Pasta Group **6-11 Servings**

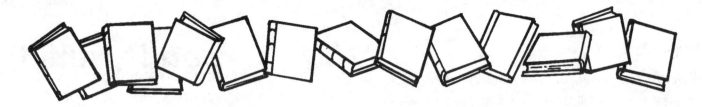

The Grouchy Ladybug

Written and Illustrated by Eric Carle

Harper & Row, 1977

Summary

An impolite ladybug wants all the aphids on the leaf instead of sharing with another ladybug. When the friendly ladybug takes up the other's offer to fight, the grouchy ladybug backs down and flies away. For the next 12 hours, the grouchy ladybug meets different members of the insect and animal kingdom, starting with a honeybee and progressing to larger animals—ending with a whale.

The grouchy ladybug bullies the various animals into fighting. However, when each accepts the challenge, the cowardly ladybug flies off. Finally, the whale uses its fin to slap the ladybug back to its original leaf. The friendly ladybug is still there. The grouchy one has learned its lesson and is happy now to share the aphids.

Hints for Reading Aloud

Use a grouchy voice whenever the grouchy ladybug speaks. Since each animal is larger than the last, you might want to lower your voice slightly and get louder for each succeeding page. You might consider counting out the time with a "bong" or "tick" sound. Use a special animal sound for each page.

What to Talk About

Ask your child some or all of the following questions:

- Why is the ladybug so grouchy?
- Who is your favorite animal that the grouchy ladybug talks to? Why is that animal your favorite?
- What makes the grouchy ladybug change its mind and become friendly at the end of the story?

Ideas and Activities

- Here is a good opportunity to introduce or reinforce information about time. If your child can count, show the numbers on the clock on each page of the story. Ask if your child sees how the hour hand changes position. If counting is a new skill, say the numbers from one to 10 or 12. If you repeat the numbers each time you read this book, your child will begin to understand that these words and symbols go together.

- Make a paper plate clock to introduce telling time. Make a clock face by writing the numbers one through 12 on a paper plate. Put a dot in the center. Use poster board to cut two hands, one shorter than the other, that look like arrows. Use a paper fastener (brad) to attach the hands at the dot. Practice telling time.

- In the story, the animals, the pages, and even the print get larger. Together, make your own variation of this type of book. Use paper that you staple on one side and then cut down on the other as in **The Grouchy Ladybug**. **Note:** Cover the staples with clear tape so fingers won't get cut. (See **How to Make Books with Children**, pages 150–152.) Tell your own story about what happens at each hour. Don't worry about the length of your book. You can add to it as your child gets older.

- Point out the position of the sun on each page and have your child notice how it changes. Explain how the sun looks like it moves in the sky as the hours of the day tick away. **Warning:** Never allow your child to look directly at the sun.

- Go outside and find some ladybugs if you can. They can be purchased at local pet stores or garden centers. This would be a good way to introduce insects since ladybugs are both colorful and harmless.

- Some of Eric Carle's wonderful stories are on video such as **The Very Hungry Caterpillar and Other Stories** (Walt Disney Home Video).

Related Reading

Bernhar, Emory. **Ladybug.** Holiday, 1992.

Carle, Eric. **The Mixed-Up Chameleon.** Harper, 1984.

Carle, Eric. **The Very Busy Spider.** Putnam, 1989.

Carle, Eric. **The Very Hungry Caterpillar.** Putnam, 1984.

Carle, Eric. **The Very Quiet Cricket.** Putnam, 1990.

Goldsen, Louise. **The Ladybug and Other Insects.** Scholastic, 1991.

Watts, Barry. **Ladybug.** Watts, 1990.

Wilhelm, Hans. **Tyrone the Horrible.** Scholastic, 1988.

Happy Birthday, Little Witch

Written by Deborah Hautzig

Illustrated by Marc Brown

Random House, 1985

Summary

Poor Little Witch is so good, never getting dirty and always eating the right foods. It is her birthday, and she is upset with her family because she knows how they will treat her. They will burst balloons, make it rain, and her mother will serve a chocolate frog cake. But Little Witch wants to celebrate her birthday with her three friends. She goes to search for them. While looking, she has some adventures. However, she returns home disappointed because she hasn't found her friends. Much to her surprise, they are waiting to help celebrate her birthday at her house.

Hints for Reading Aloud

This book begins on an upbeat note and should be read that way until Little Witch gets discouraged and complains about her birthday. Then her voice should sound discouraged. When Mother Witch screeches at Little Witch, read the lines in a screeching voice. Each time Little Witch says a magic spell, get the rhythm and the rhyme. Your child may enjoy saying these with you so repeat them a few times. Make Little Witch sound sad as she realizes that nothing is going right for her birthday. Have everyone sound happy at her party. When her mother presents her with a gift of dirt, make both of them delighted. Read the line "I LOVE YOU ANYWAY" with lots of love in your voice and give your child a big hug. When they all sing "Happy Birthday," you and your child can sing it too.

What to Talk About

- This story doesn't take place at Halloween, but ask your child why it might still be a good one to read at that time of year.

- What makes Little Witch different from her family? What makes you think she loves them and they love her even if they are different?

- Have you ever been to a birthday party or had one? What did you like most?

- What things in the book couldn't really happen? What things could?

- What things happen that make Little Witch feel so bad about herself that she calls herself a flop? Do you ever have times that you feel bad about the things that you do? How can you help yourself feel better about them?

Ideas and Activities

- Little Witch's friends are all dressed in costumes. With your child, play dress-up. This is easily accomplished with some old hats, shoes, and jewelry. Of course, you can get much more elaborate, adding any article of clothing that you have around that might be fun. If you don't already have a dress-up bag or box, this is a great opportunity to create one. This will encourage your child to use his or her imagination when creating various characters.

- Nasty Witch says candy is good. Find out about what candy can really do to your teeth and in simple terms explain it to your child. Then take some time to explain why brushing teeth is so important, especially after eating candy or other sweets.

- Play party games. Pin the Tail on the Donkey is a classic and can usually be found at party stores. You can create your own version called Pin the Nose on the Clown. Find a picture of a clown and cut out red circles from construction paper for the noses. Hang the picture on a wall. Put tape on the back of the red noses. Blindfold the children, turn them around, give them noses, and then point them in the direction of the clown. They should try to get the nose in the right place. Be aware that many young children will not play a game that involves a blindfold. Don't insist that they participate.

- Bake a cake with your child. You can make one from scratch or try a cake mix. Let your child do as much as possible. Decorate the cake together, discussing first how you will do it. You may find that skipping the baking altogether and going right on to decorating is a better idea for you and your child. In that case, buy a prepared cake, a can of icing, and some cake decorations.

- Think about Little Witch's names for her pets—Bow-Wow, the cat, and Scrubby, the dog. Think about names for pets that might make people think the animal is something other than it is. Make a list of these.

- Little Witch has all kinds of spells even though they don't work. With your child make up some spells, even though they won't work. These can be for things like making the bed or putting away toys.

Related Reading

Hautzig, Deborah. **Little Witch's Night Out.** Random, 1984.

Stevenson, James. **Yuck!** Morrow, 1984.

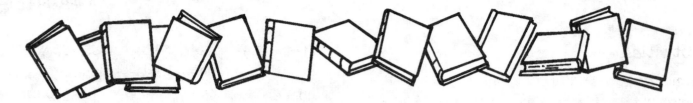

If You Give a Mouse a Cookie

Written by Laura Joffe Numeroff

Illustrated by Felicia Bond

Harper & Row, 1985

Summary

In this short book, a boy imagines what would happen if one were to give a mouse a cookie. The mouse gets his cookies and then needs milk and all the other things that might go with it. The demanding little mouse wears out his host and brings everything around to a full circle.

Hints for Reading Aloud

Since this story builds upon itself, get more involved as you read each page. You can sound more exasperated with each of the mouse's demands, but be sure to always do it in an amusing way.

What to Talk About

Ask your child some or all of the following questions:

- What is it that the mouse really wants?
- Could this story really happen? Why or why not?
- What other stories have famous mice in them?
- Why do you think mice are characters in so many stories?
- What do you think might really happen if you gave a mouse a cookie?
- What would have happened in the story if the mouse hadn't been given the cookie?

Ideas and Activities

- Drink some milk and eat some cookies with your child. Look in a mirror together to see if either of you has a "milk mustache."

- Give your child paper and crayons to draw a picture for you. Provide a pen for your child to sign his or her name. When the picture is finished, make sure to hang it in a place of honor on your refrigerator, like the mouse in the story.

- Find out about real mice. The mouse in this story ate a cookie. What do real mice eat? Are cookies part of their diets?

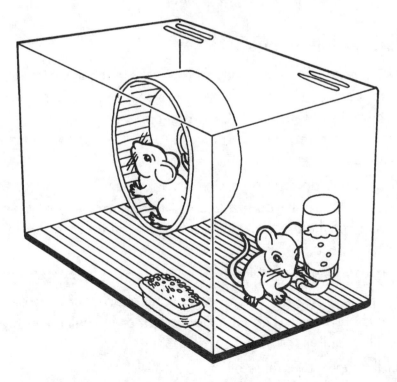

- A mouse is usually pretty small. Look at the pictures in the story. What kinds of things does the mouse fit into because he is so small? With your child name things you would both like to fit into but can't because you are so much bigger than a mouse.

- Together with your child create a variation for this story. Start with the opening line "If you give a mouse a cookie , . . . "and fill in some other things that might happen. For example, "If you give a mouse a cookie, he may break it into tiny pieces and scatter them all over the room."

- Look at the pictures in the book. With your child find all the familiar objects that you have in your house. Are there other scenes from the book, such as the objects on the refrigerator, that are familiar to you?

- Read **If You Give a Moose a Muffin** also by Laura Joffe Numeroff. (See the **Related Reading** below.)

- Compare the two stories. Which did your child like better? (The answer will be revealed by how many times your child asks you to read each one.)

Related Reading

Larrick, Nancy, ed. **Mice Are Nice.** Putnam, 1990.

Numeroff, Laura Joffe. **If You Give a Moose a Muffin.** Harper, 1991.

Ormondroyd, Edward. **Broderick.** Houghton, 1969.

Potter, Beatrix. **The Tale of Mrs. Tittlemouse and Other Mouse Stories.** Warner, 1985.

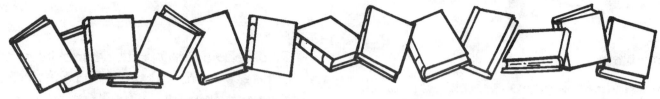

If You Made a Million

Written by David M. Schwartz

Illustrated by Steven Kellogg

Lothrop, Lee and Shepard, 1989

Summary

Making a million dollars seems like a simple task as one reads this easy-to-understand book about money. Building on the concept of earning, beginning with a penny and progressing through coins and dollars, the reader starts to have a simple understanding of money. The concept of interest is explained as is the system of checks. The whimsical illustrations enhance the story while pictures of real money make the book practical for showing children pictures of the various denominations.

Hints for Reading Aloud

Many lines in this book are written using all capital letters with exclamation points at the ends of the sentences. Read these in a loud, excited voice. For the pages that explain the coins, show real coins and explain the combinations. Depending on the age of your child, you may want to read these and point out or count the coins while reading.

When you are reading the equivalents such as "one five-dollar bill or five one-dollar bills," you will want to pause at the "or" and let your child think about the same amounts of money created in different ways.

What to Talk About

- This book has useful notes from the author located at the back of the book. They answer many questions posed in the book and provide good background information for you before you read the book aloud and discuss it with your child.

- The most obvious question to ask your child is "What would you do if you made a million dollars?" Ask your child how he or she would rather be paid—with dimes, nickels, etc.

- How does your child think people earn money?

- Explain that the ogre is a grouchy character. Does your child think the job of ogre-tamer is really worth a million dollars? Why or why not?

- Talk about the value of money.

Ideas and Activities

- This book presents a myriad of opportunities concerning money. Several activities are described on this page . Choose those that are appropriate for your child's level and interest. You may wish to obtain real or play money before beginning. **Warning:** Children should never put real or play money in their mouths or ears.

- With your child, think about something that might come in a million other than money. Make a list. Together, see if you might be able to contemplate how much space a million of one object might take. For instance, if you were to put a million one-inch squares on a wall, how much wall space would you need?

- Count out pennies, nickels, or dimes. Determine how high you need to count. A young child may only count to three. An older child may count to over 100.

- Find out the cost of something that your child has or would like to have. Show how much the item costs by counting out that amount of money.

- Stack some coins. Have your child guess how many coins are in the stack. Then count them together. You may also wish to have your child guess how much the stack of coins is worth and then figure out the value together.

- Let your child earn money to clarify the concept of "working for pay." Find a few simple tasks that are appropriate for your child's age and skill level. Decide how much you will pay for these jobs. Help your child choose what to do with the money. Explain that all of the money can be saved or spent, or part of the money can be saved and part of it spent.

- Show your child the picture of a check in the book. Explain checks using simple terms. Tell why people don't want to carry large amounts of cash or send it through the mail. You may want to show your child an actual check from your checkbook.

- With older children, do some money equivalency problems. For instance, give your child two dimes and five pennies. See if he or she can convert this amount into a quarter or five nickels. Make sure you have the change available to choose from for this activity. You can even use a sheet of paper with a large equals sign and place one set of coins on the left and a stack to choose from on the right.

Related Reading

Adams, Barbara J. **The Go-Around Dollar.** Macmillan, 1992.

Viorst, Judith. **Alexander, Who Used to Be Rich Last Sunday.** Macmillan, 1978.

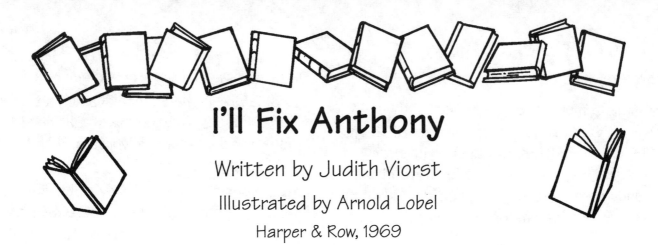

I'll Fix Anthony

Written by Judith Viorst

Illustrated by Arnold Lobel

Harper & Row, 1969

Summary

The boy telling this story is treated badly by his older brother, Anthony. Anthony will not read to him or play with him. Anthony thinks he stinks. The younger brother dreams about the time "when I'm six [and] I'll fix Anthony." He plans to have a dog who will bite Anthony. He will go to the baseball games, flower shows, and the movies by himself because Anthony will be sick. He'll be bigger, stronger, and more intelligent than Anthony. He will win all the games, and Anthony will cry. All that will happen when he is six.

Hints for Reading Aloud

Emphasize the words that show how mean Anthony is so his little brother's plans seem understandable. Emphasize the "opposite words" which show the differences—"float/sink," "tall/short," and the adjectives which show superiority—"faster, higher."

Anthony's antics should sound mean, but the younger brother's should sound fair. The last page should be read with a giggle.

What to Talk About

- The younger brother is upset with Anthony. Should he be upset? Which is the funniest way he will "fix Anthony"? Do you think he will be able to do all these things to Anthony?
- What is special about being an older brother or sister? Are there any problems with being the oldest?
- What is special about being the younger brother or sister? Are there any problems with being the youngest?
- Can your child relate this story to his or her own life with older and/or younger siblings?

Ideas and Activities

- Find a book of names at the library. Look up the name "Anthony." What does it mean? Where did it come from? Find a good name for the younger brother.

- In the book of names, look up your child's name. What does it mean? Does your child like its meaning? Where does it come from? Check out your name, the names of your other children, and the names of your children's best friends.

- Ask your child about age and adulthood. What is the best age to be? Why is that the perfect age? At what age will you be an adult? What does it mean to be an adult? Then have your child draw a picture of some things that he or she will be able to do as an adult that cannot be done now. Your child might have fun asking family members and friends what they think is the perfect age. If possible, let your child do this independently. Later, ask what he or she found out.

- Have your child ask some older relatives, including yourself, how they got along with their brothers and sisters when they were younger. Encourage your child to tell these people the story of **I'll Fix Anthony** and see if they ever felt this way.

- There are many antonyms (opposites) in this book. Play a game of opposites with your child. When you say "up," your child should say "down." An older child may be able to give you the words for which you say the opposites. This is an amusing game and easily played while riding in the car.

Related Reading

Blume, Judy. **The Pain and the Great One.** Macmillan, 1984.

Kellogg, Steven. **Much Bigger Than Martin.** Dial, 1976.

Latkin, Patricia. **Don't Touch My Room.** Little, 1988.

Little, Jean. **Jess Was the Brave One.** Viking, 1992.

Tyler, Linda W. **My Brother Thinks He Knows It All.** Puffin, 1991.

Viorst, Judith. **Alexander and the Terrible, Horrible, No Good, Very Bad Day.** Macmillan, 1972.

Viorst, Judith. **Rosie and Michael.** Macmillan, 1974.

Yaccarino, Dan. **Big Brother Mike.** Hyperion, 1993.

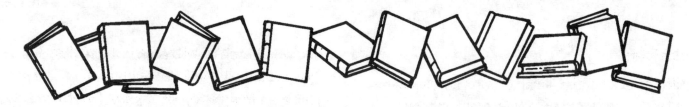

The Important Book

Written by Margaret Wise Brown

Illustrated by Leonard Weisgard

Harper and Row, 1949

Summary

The Important Book tells about all kinds of things that are important and the reasons for their importance. Each page includes something else that could be considered important. None of the things talked about are earth shattering discoveries but are all rather the ordinary, everyday kinds of things that we encounter in our lives.

Hints for Reading Aloud

This book has a repetitive language pattern. Each page begins with "The important thing about...." Thus the pages, while short, will be monotonous if all read the same way. Notice that the type on each page changes. Let the size of the type be your guide in reading. If you read a page that has large type, make your voice sound big. For pages with smaller type, make your voice sound smaller. As an alternative, you may wish to choose what you find is most important and really emphasize that.

What to Talk About

Ask your child some or all of the following questions:

- What things are really important to you? Why?
- Why do you think the author chose the things she did to write about?
- Which of the items that are written about would you also agree are important?

Ideas and Activities

- With your child, draw or paint a picture of one thing that is important. Underneath, write or have your child write what it is and why it's important.

- Find five to ten important items in your house. Adjust the number depending on your child's age. These might be items like a hairbrush or spoon. Place them in a bag. Give a clue about an item's importance, such as "We keep our hair neat with this." Let your child guess what the object is. If guessed correctly, take the item out of the bag. If guessed incorrectly, give more clues. Depending on your child's age, give him or her a chance to choose an item and let you guess what it is.

- Choose something that you both think is important. It might be a trip to the beach or helping a sick neighbor. Determine why both of you think it is important. If it is something you can do, then do it together. If not, then talk about it.

- Make something with your child. It might be a block tower, a simple wood project, or cookies. Leave something out that would be important but can easily be replaced. For example, leave out the chips from chocolate chip cookies. Help your child realize that something important is missing. Determine what it is. Decide what might happen if the important thing is not added. Depending on how you think your child will react, leave the important thing out and complete the project. Then try it again, including the important thing. Compare the two versions. **Warning:** Be sure you only try this with something that will be safe without the important thing.

- Write an innovation of a page from **The Important Book** for someone special. An innovation uses the story as a model but is completed with your own words. Here is an example: "The important thing about my grandmother is that she loves me. She is a good cook. She makes me laugh. She reads good stories. But the important thing about my grandmother is that she loves me." Then add illustrations.

Related Reading

Denslow, Sharon P. **At Taylor's Place.** Macmillan, 1990.

Greenberg, Melanie S. **My Father's Luncheonette.** Dutton, 1991.

Kuklin, Susan. **Going to My Ballet Class.** Macmillan, 1989.

Mansell, Dom. **My Old Teddy.** Candlewick, 1992.

Rockwell, Anne, and Harlow Rockwell. **I Play in My Room.** Macmillan, 1981.

Van Leeuwen, Jean. **Emma Bean.** Dial, 1993.

Wilson, Beth P. **Jenny.** Macmillan, 1990.

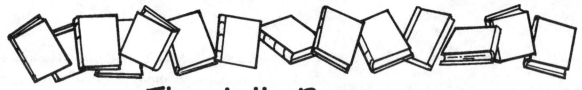

The Jolly Postman
(or Other People's Letters)

Written and Illustrated by Janet and Allan Ahlberg

Little, Brown and Company, 1986

Summary

A postman (mailman) delivers letters to well-known fairy tale characters, including Cinderella, the Three Bears, and Jack's Giant. (The letter each receives is included in its own envelope.) The postman is offered tea at each house, although he doesn't drink the green liquid offered by the Wicked Witch. After a birthday party at Goldilocks' house, he returns home for yet another cup of tea.

Hints for Reading Aloud

There is no dialogue in the story, but three letters are written by famous fairy tale characters or their lawyers! Goldilocks' letter to the Three Bears should sound "regretful." Jack's letter to the giant should sound "boastful." Little Red Riding Hood's lawyer writes a letter in a threatening tone. Have fun!

What to Talk About

- Your child will know most, if not all, of the stories referred to in this book. Ask your child to retell these in her or his own words.

- Discuss what might happen in other fairy tales following the ending "happily ever after."

- This is a very funny book, and it's important that your child is aware that books can be humorous. Ask what other books have made your child laugh.

- Does your child like receiving mail? What particular type of mail, if any, does she or he look forward to receiving?

Ideas and Activities

- Have your child learn a joke or two to tell at family gatherings. This is a great way to develop a sense of humor. A classic knock-knock joke follows.

Knock, knock.	Who's there?
Banana.	Banana who?
Knock, knock.	Who's there?
Banana.	Banana who?
Knock, knock.	Who's there?
Banana.	Banana who?
Knock, knock.	Who's there?
Orange.	Orange who?

  Orange you glad I didn't say banana again?

- Find other humorous books at the library and read them together.
- Take a trip to the local post office and ask for a short tour. Both you and your child will find it interesting to learn all the steps a letter goes through.
- Use the book to introduce what an address is. Write your address. Then explain that each family and business in the world has a different address.
- Try to be at your mailbox when the postal carrier is putting the mail in it. Let your child take out the mail. Here is another opportunity to point out your address.

- Have your child make a card for a relative and put a stamp on the envelope. Ask the relative to correspond with your child or call to say that she or he got the card.

- Read the fairy tales that are mentioned in the story. Even if your child knows them, they can be a joy to reread. Perhaps you can find a different version than you ordinarily read and share the new artwork with your child.

Related Reading

Ahlberg, Janet and Allan. **The Jolly Christmas Postman.** Little, 1991.

Buchnall, Caroline. **The Three Little Pigs.** Dial, 1987.

Galdone, Paul. **The Three Bears; The Three Little Pigs.** Houghton, 1979.

Marshall, James. **Goldilocks and the Three Bears.** Dial, 1988.

Perrault, Charles. **Cinderella.** Little, 1992. (Retold by Barbara Karlin, 1992.)

Perrault, Charles. **Cinderella or the Little Glass Slipper.** Puffin, 1977.

Quackenbush, Robert. **Robert Quackenbush's Treasury of Humor.** Doubleday, 1992.

Ross, Tony, Reteller. **Goldilocks and the Three Bears.** Viking, 1992.

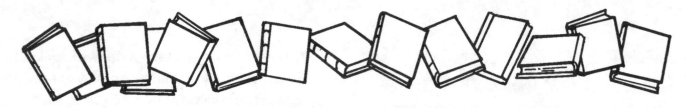

Katy and the Big Snow

 Written and Illustrated by Virginia Lee Burton

Houghton Mifflin, 1943

Summary

Katy is a huge red tractor. She is able to be a bulldozer and a snowplow. She never slows down until the work is done. If there are small jobs, Katy can stay in her house at the highway department. However, when no one else is big or strong enough to do the work, the city calls for Katy. One winter, the snow came down in huge amounts. The entire town came to a standstill. Everyone called for Katy to help, including the police and fire departments. Katy worked very hard that day. She continued to work until the entire town was moving again.

Hints for Reading Aloud

Make the police chief, postmaster, and others sound desperate when they ask Katy for help. Katy should sound caring and confident when answering. Be sure to make the "chugging" sound when indicated in the story. Have your child make the sound with you. Make Katy's last "chugging" noises sound slow and tired.

What to Talk About

- If you live in a place where it snows, talk about what kinds of activities you can do in the snow and what kinds of activities the snow can keep you from doing.

- If your child hasn't seen snow or doesn't remember seeing it, talk about how cold it is and tell about making a snowman or going sledding.

- Talk about the jobs different vehicles do.

Ask your child some or all of the following questions:

- How is a truck different from a car?

- What does a fire truck look like?

- Is there a person you know who works very hard and never quits? How is this person like Katy?

- How did Katy feel after her day of plowing?

Ideas and Activities

- Remind your child about Katy the next time you see a snowplow or bulldozer doing its job. How does the equipment look like Katy? Is it the same color?

- If you can find a storage area for road equipment, visit it. Cities often have utility yards. You might be able to arrange a tour through a city department.

- Notice how the town is drawn in the book. Do you live in a similar area? Do you live in the city or the country? Get some books from the library that show different places where people live. Have your child compare and contrast the pictures with your house and community.

- Play in the sandbox or the dirt with your child. If you have some toy plows or dump trucks, level off the dirt and remove it with them. If you don't, use a toy trowel to do this. Have fun digging holes in the sand.

- Obtain the computer software version of Virginia L. Burton's classic children's story: **Mike Mulligan and His Steam Shovel** by Houghton Mifflin Interactive. CD-ROM for MAC and PC. Available from Educorp, 7434 Trade Street, San Diego, CA 92121-2410. 1-800-843-9497.

Related Reading

Burton, Virginia L. **The Little House.** Houghton, 1942, 1978.

Burton, Virginia L. **Mike Mulligan and His Steam Shovel.** Houghton, 1939.

Gramatsky, Hardie. **Little Toot.** Putnam, 1939.

Lenski, Lois. **Little Auto.** McKay, 1980.

Piper, Watty. **The Little Engine That Could.** Putnam, 1930.

Swuft, Hildegarde, and Lynd Ward. **Little Red Lighthouse and the Great Grey Bridge.** Harcourt, 1942.

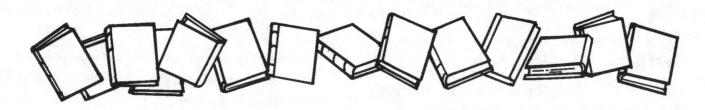

Kitty's Colors

Written by Dick McCue

Illustrated by Lisa McCue

Simon and Schuster, 1983

Summary

This charming book is all about Kitty's crayons. For each color in her box of crayons, a rhyme describes several objects found that are that color. Kitty holds an oversized crayon so readers can easily see the color the rhyme is describing.

Hints for Reading Aloud

The story is all done in rhyme. Read each page as a separate poem. Let your child chime in with the name of the color as you show the page. Before long, your youngster will be calling out "blue" or "purple" at the right time.

What to Talk About

- Ask what your child's favorite color is. A very young child may not yet know the names of colors. In that case, talk about different colors and some objects that are associated with them, such as a yellow sun or a green tree.
- Ask what your child thinks of Kitty.

Ideas and Activities

- Get a box of crayons and drawing paper. Depending on your child's age, you may opt for a box that holds only eight crayons. Take out each crayon, show it to your child, and name the color. Now invite your child to color a picture.

- Let your child try another medium to experience color. Markers are the least messy. Tempera, water colors, and finger paints tend to be messy. **Note:** Your child can paint while sitting in the bathtub. This makes cleanup a snap.

- Get some food coloring. Show your child what happens when you mix the colors together in water, milk, or white frosting. Follow the directions on the box of food coloring to get the colors they suggest, or feel free to experiment. **Warning:** Food coloring stains so decide where you want to do this before beginning.

- Make green crowns for you and your child by cutting pointed edges out of green construction paper. Tape as many pieces together as you need to fit around each head. Decorate the pieces.

- Kitty sees objects of each color. Find a crayon that matches one of those colors. Then go on a color hunt around your house. Make a list of objects that are that particular color. Then try another color. Which color has the greatest number of objects? Which has the least?

- Let your child use crayons to decorate paper lunch bags or trick-or-treat bags.

- Kitty tastes purple jelly. Let your child taste purple jelly. Look at other types of jelly and jam at the store. Ask your child to name the colors.

- Point out any buses you see. Explain the difference between yellow school buses and other buses. This is a good time to talk about riding a school bus.

- Have a color meal. For instance, if you choose green, wear green clothing, use green napkins, and eat green foods such as pea soup, lettuce, and green apples.

- With your child use sidewalk chalk and make a rainbow. Make it large and give each child, if others are present, a different color to fill in after you do the outline.

Related Reading

Bond, Michael. **Paddington's Colors.** (Series: **Paddington**) Viking, 1991.

De Brunhoff, Laurent. **Babar's Book of Color.** Random, 1984.

Dodds, Dayle Ann. **The Color Box.** Little, 1992.

Ehlert, Lois. **Color Zoo.** Harper, 1989.

Hoban, Tana. **Of Colors and Things.** Greenwillow, 1989.

Sharratt, Nick. **The Green Quilt.** Candlewick, 1992.

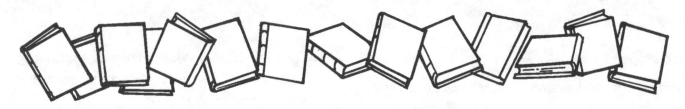

Latkes and Applesauce

Written by Fran Manushkin

Illustrated by Robin Spowart

Scholastic, 1990

Summary

In a small Eastern European village long ago, a poor family prepares to celebrate Hanukkah. A horrible blizzard arrives on the first night and covers the potatoes so there can be no latkes (potato pancakes). There are no apples either, for the bad weather made the crop very small. The family sings a song and tries to celebrate with soup. Soon there are two visitors—a wet orange kitten and a starving dog. The young children, Rebecca and Ezra, ask their parents to take these poor creatures in and, in the spirit of Hanukkah, the dog and cat find a home. The family continues throughout the holiday without the traditional foods. However, on the eighth and last night a miracle occurs. The dog

runs out to dig in the snow and uncovers potatoes. The cat climbs a tree and finds some snow-covered apples. As the family sits down to eat, Ezra declares he will name the dog "Latkes," for he found the potatoes, and Rebecca says she will name the cat "Applesauce," for she found the apples.

Hints for Reading Aloud

Here is a family who has seen hardship but are happy with one another. Hanukkah is a holiday they have been looking forward to all year. They should sound enthusiastic even in the face of adversity.

What to Talk About

- The spirit of Hanukkah is sharing time with the family. Point out that the Menashe family does not exchange gifts. Their love of the holiday is reflected in their taking in the cat and dog. Ask what your child thinks is the importance of Hanukkah.

Ideas and Activities

- Follow the latke recipe from the back of the book or use the one that follows.

Warning: The frying should be done by an adult. Use extreme caution.

Latkes

Ingredients: 3 potatoes, 2 teaspoons (10 mL) grated onion, 1 egg, 6 tablespoons (90 mL) flour, 4 tablespoons (60 mL) oil

Directions: Wash, peel, and grate the potatoes. Drain them in a colander. Mix in the grated onion, egg, and flour. Heat the oil in a skillet. Drop one tablespoon (15 mL) of the potato mixture at a time into the oil. Use a spatula to turn over the latkes so they brown on both sides. Remove them from the pan, and drain them on a paper towel. Serve them warm with sour cream or applesauce.

- The dog is called "Latkes" and the cat "Applesauce." If you have a pet, how did you choose its name? If you don't have a pet, what are names you could use?

- Learn more about the holiday of Hanukkah. (See the **Related Reading**.)

- Dreidels are available at many stores in December. Find one and play this ancient game by following the directions in the book.

- Make a marshmallow menorah (candle holder). You need a rectangular piece of cardboard covered with aluminum foil, 10 large and 9 small marshmallows, frosting, and 9 birthday candles. On the bottoms of 9 large marshmallows, place a dab of frosting. Stick them onto the cardboard. On the last marshmallow, use frosting to stick a second large marshmallow on top for the shamus, or leader. Put frosting in the middle of each small marshmallow. Place one on top of each large marshmallow. Stick a candle in each holder. Use extreme caution in lighting this menorah.

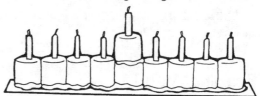

- Potatoes are root vegetables. Find out how root vegetables grow. What other vegetables are part of this group? Compare potatoes to carrots and turnips.

Related Reading

Chaikin, Miriam. **Light Another Candle: The Story and Meaning of Hanukkah.** Clarion Books/Ticknor and Fields, 1981.

Ehrlich, Amy. **The Story of Hanukkah.** Dial, 1989.

Kimmel, Eric A. **Hershel and the Hanukkah Goblins.** Holiday House, 1989.

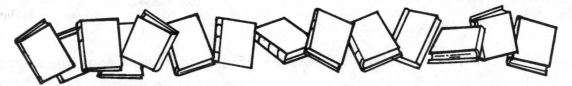

The Little Engine That Could

Retold by Watty Piper

Illustrated by Ruth Sanderson

Platt & Monk, 1930

Summary

This is the classic children's story about believing in yourself. When the happy little train filled with wondrous things for children can't go one more inch, it is the Little Blue Engine with its timeless refrain, "I think I can—I think I can," who comes to the rescue and saves the day.

Hints for Reading Aloud

This story lends itself to a delightful repetition with the "I think I can" line. Children will enjoy the story as you take on the voices of the trains. Invite them to chant along as you huff and puff up the hills, letting your voice show your strength and determination. Make sure that you speed up the repetition of the Little Blue Engine.

Each of the engines has its own personality. The Shiny New Engine is haughty, the Big Strong Engine is indignant, the Rusty Old Engine is tired, and the Little Blue Engine is kindly. As you read each part, take on the personality of that particular train.

This story has many onomatopoeic words. These are words that imitate sounds. Words such as chug, puffed, ding-dong, snorted, and bellowed fall into this category. When you come to this type of word, emphasize the sound it makes. Sometimes you might even want to replace the word with an actual sound, such as ringing a bell to replace ding-dong.

What to Talk About

Ask your child some or all of the following questions:

- What did the Little Engine accomplish?
- How did the Little Engine meet the challenge?
- What challenges have you had to face?
- Have you ever felt like the Little Engine?
- Have you been on a train? Tell about it. If you haven't, what do you think it would be like?

Ideas and Activities

- Read other train stories. See the **Related Reading** for suggestions.

- Find out more about some of the train terms mentioned in the book. These include switching trains in the yard, parlor cars, and berths.

- Play Choo Choo Train. It can be done with two people, but it works better with more. Line up front to back. Have each person hold the shoulders of the person in front of him or her. The engineer is the person at the front. He or she blows the whistle and decides when and where the train goes.

- If possible, take a train trip. Amusement parks, fairs, carnivals, and even malls may provide small trains to give your child the opportunity to go for a ride.

- With your child, name some of the things the train is carrying. Have your child compare some of the toys to ones that he or she has. Look at the good things to eat. Which foods would your child like to eat?

- Explain that this book was written long ago. Look for unfamiliar words. For example, bobbed hair is hair that is cut short, or a berth is a bed on a train.

- Each engine had a reason why it couldn't pull the train over the mountain. However, the Little Blue Engine thought she could and she did. Tell your child about an experience that you had in which you really didn't know if you could be successful, but you were. Ask your child to set a goal that is attainable with some work. It might even be something that you want to achieve together, such as learning to play checkers or planting a garden. Reread **The Little Engine That Could** as inspiration when you or your child need a lift.

- Watch the video **The Little Engine That Could** (MCA Home Video, 1991).

Related Reading

Ardizzone, Edward. **Little Tim and the Brave Sea Captain.** Puffin, 1983.

Armstrong, Jennifer. **Hugh Can Do.** Crown, 1992.

Crews, Donald. **Freight Train.** Greenwillow, 1978.

Gerrard, Roy. **Rosie and the Rustlers.** Farrar, 1989.

Gibbons, Gail. **Trains.** Holiday, 1987.

Kanetzke, Howard. **Trains and Railroads.** Raintree, 1978.

Olsen, Arielle North. **The Lighthouse Keeper's Daughter.** Little, 1987.

Steig, William. **Brave Irene.** Farrar, 1986.

Weisner, David. **Hurricane.** Houghton, 1990.

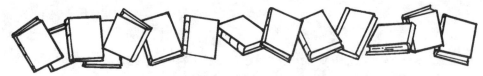

The Little House

Written and Illustrated by Virginia Lee Burton

Scholastic, 1942

Summary

In this story, the Little House begins her life in the country. As so often happens, the city eventually grows and moves out to the country. The Little House who loves the seasons and the sound of the countryside is soon engulfed with the sights and sounds of the city. The Little House unhappily endures changes from horseless carriages to skyscrapers. Then one day she is rediscovered by the granddaughter of one of her former occupants. The Little House is moved and once again becomes a happy little house in the country.

Hints for Reading Aloud

The Little House has a personality that the author conveys through words and pictures. When she is first in the country, she is happy and carefree. Convey this in your reading by sounding lighthearted. As the city moves in around her, she becomes upset. Let your voice portray this. Soon no one cares about the Little House. For this part of the story, sound as if you don't even know who the Little House is. When the granddaughter of the little girl who first lived in the house finds her, show a bit of surprise but great happiness, especially as the Little House is transported to her new location in the country.

This book may be a bit long for little children, so you may want to read it over more than one sitting. The first break seems to come after the seasons have been described. The next logical break comes with the appearance of the great great-granddaughter of the man who built the house.

What to Talk About

- What has happened to the house? Why does she want to move? Usually when we think about moving, we think about people going other places. What makes this story different from others about moving?

- Talk about the difference between city and country life. What changes take place to convert one to the other? Discuss with your child where you live now. If you have lived both in the city and the country, tell about your experiences. Where would your child prefer to live—the city or the country?

- The Little House lived through different seasons. Talk about seasons and which one you like best. What activities are unique to each season?

Ideas and Activities

- The Little House goes through lots of changes in her surroundings. With your child, walk in your neighborhood and point out changes. Depending on where you live, these might be new buildings or a new bird nest in a tree. Then give your child an opportunity to find changes in your neighborhood.

- There are many types of transportation mentioned in the story, such as a horseless carriage and a trolley. List all the types of transportation mentioned in the story. Read some books about them. If possible find pictures or models of some of the older forms of transportation.

- Find out how houses are built. Try visiting a new housing project and talking to people. Otherwise, read some books. What kinds of jobs are there for people who build houses? (carpenters, plumbers, electricians, etc.)

- Build a house together. This can be made from cards, but these are much tougher to make than they seem. You might use building blocks or try real woodworking. As always, exercise extreme caution with any project you undertake.

- Depending on the season when you read the story, discuss special projects you do around the house.

Examples: If you live where it snows, you might put up storm windows. If you live where it's hot, you might check the air conditioner to be sure it works. Let your child see what house maintenance is all about.

- Find out about some different kinds of houses people use. Not everyone lives in a little house. Look in the real estate section of your local newspaper to find different types of housing in your neighborhood. You can extend this by determining what types of homes animals have.

- The Little House got new windows and shutters to look fresh again. Choose a small project with your child to help beautify your house. This can be as easy as straightening books on a shelf or as elaborate as planting a new flower bed together.

Related Reading

Ackerman, Karen. **This Old House.** Macmillan, 1992.

Beck, Martine. **The Rescue of Brown Bear and White Bear.** Little, 1991.

Dragonwagon, Crescent. **Home Place.** Macmillan, 1990.

Hoberman, Mary Ann. **A House Is a House for Me.** Viking, 1978.

McNaughton, Colin. **Who's That Banging on the Ceiling?** Candlewick, 1992.

Pfanner, Louise. **Louise Builds a House.** Orchard, 1989.

Shulevitz, Uri. **One Monday Morning.** Macmillan, 1986.

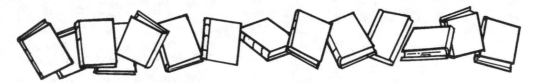

Love You Forever

Written by Robert Munsch

Illustrated by Sheila McGraw

Firefly Books, 1986

Summary

This books shows the passage of time. A mother rocks her son and sings a special song to him when he is an infant, a two-year-old, a nine-year-old, a teenager, and young man. When the mother is too old and frail to finish the song, the son picks her up, rocks her, and sings the song to her. He realizes his mother will soon no longer be around to comfort him. The son then goes into his baby daughter's room, picks her up, and continues the family song with the next generation.

Hints for Reading Aloud

Since it is a song, invent a melody for the four lines. Don't be concerned if you can't carry a tune. A young child will not care about the quality of your singing voice but will be delighted with hearing you sing.

Enjoy the illustrations with your child. Ask if it looks funny to see the mother rocking her grown son.

There is a cat in almost every illustration. Find them. Notice the pictures of the son as he grows up.

What to Talk About

- Discuss what the ladder is doing on the top of the car.

- Ask about the different people in your family. Have your child tell who each person is, naming them from youngest to oldest. List as many family members as possible, including grandparents, aunts, uncles, cousins, and the immediate family. Discuss how these people are related to your child.

- The song mentions the words love and like. What does your child think the difference is between these two words?

- With an older child you might want to discuss family traditions. What do you look forward to that the family does every week? every summer or winter? on a special holiday?

Ideas and Activities

- Sing some of your family's favorite songs. If you don't have any, ask your child to name songs that he or she knows. Encourage the family to sing one or more of these songs. Singing is a great way to pass time while in the car. Build up a whole repertoire.

- How about a family drawing done by your child? Let your child express his or her artistic side by composing a picture of the family, including parents and siblings. You can offer help, but do not force the issue if your child doesn't want or need it. By all means compliment the finished product. Your child's artistic talent will bloom only if loved ones praise his or her efforts. Your youngster might not be a Rembrandt, but he or she will go farther if given lots of encouragement.

- Have your child make a connection with a senior citizen in your community. This can be a relative, but it doesn't have to be. You might be fortunate enough to have a neighbor who is willing to talk to your child about the "old days." If not, you might need to find a senior citizens center. See if you and your child can spend some time visiting with a senior buddy. If your child has not spent much time around older people, this might be an eye-opening experience.

- Share photos of your child, starting, if possible, from when he or she was born. Together, sequence the pictures in order from when your child was the youngest to the most current. If you have the photos labeled and in albums, share this progression of growth with your child by looking at the pictures in order.

Related Reading

Ackerman, Karen. **I Know a Place.** Houghton, 1992.

Alexander, Martha. **Where Does the Sky End, Grandpa?** Harcourt, 1992.

Baynton, Martin. **Why Do You Love Me?** Greenwillow, 1990.

Eisenberg, Phyllis R. **You're My Nikki.** Dial, 1992.

Hazen, Barbara S. **Even If I Did Something Awful?** Macmillan, 1992.

Hudson, Wade. **I Love My Family.** Scholastic, 1993.

Johnson, Angela. **When I Am Old With You.** Orchard, 1990.

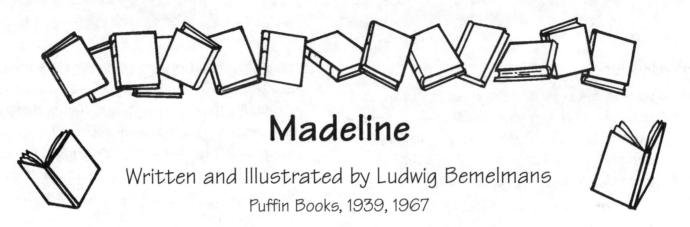

Madeline

Written and Illustrated by Ludwig Bemelmans

Puffin Books, 1939, 1967

Summary

Written in rhyme, the story of Madeline is one of a little girl who lives in a boarding school in France. Madeline is the littlest in a group of a dozen girls all identically dressed. But Madeline distinguishes herself because she is not afraid of mice, and she knows how to scare the devoted Miss Clavel better than anyone else by needing to have her appendix taken out in the middle of the night. Her classmates' visit to the hospital and Madeline's resulting scar from the surgery bring about a satisfying ending to this story. For decades this story's gentle humor has entranced children with its drawing of various sights in Paris, including the Eiffel Tower.

Hints for Reading Aloud

Madeline is written in rhyme. Read the lines to the period before stopping, although you will want to pause at the ends of the lines. When you read Miss Clavel's line "Something is not right," stop and wait a moment before going on. Toward the end of the book, when Miss Clavel runs faster and faster, emphasize those words and say them faster and faster. Say her words to the children with real concern in your voice. On the last page lower your voice to a whisper.

What to Talk About

- **Madeline** gives modern children a glimpse of what boarding school in an earlier era might have been like. If your child does not know what boarding school is, explain it. Ask if your child might enjoy going to boarding school someday.

- Madeline is really a very sick little girl. Talk to your child about being seriously ill. How does it feel? Explain a bit about appendicitis and what the surgery might be like. After your child has a better understanding, ask if he or she would really want a scar like Madeline's.

- Discuss visiting someone in the hospital. What might it be like? What would be an appropriate gift to bring? What gifts did Madeline receive?

- **Madeline** takes place in Paris. Discuss some of the interesting places to visit there. What makes Paris different from your hometown? What places has your child heard about that he or she would like to see?

Ideas and Activities

- Ludwig Bemelmans wrote and illustrated the story. Look carefully, and you will see pictures of Paris, including the Eiffel Tower and Notre Dame. Together look at a world map and find Paris, France. With an older child, try to estimate how many miles it is from your home to Paris. Compare pictures of Paris from a book or travel brochure to the ones in the story. Can your child find some famous sights?

- There are twelve little girls in the story. Talk about the concept of a dozen. Find examples around your house of things that are a dozen. The most likely place is in the kitchen. Do you have a dozen eggs or a dozen cookies? Count the items.

- The girls are dressed in uniforms. Talk about the pros and cons of wearing school uniforms. Compile a list of occupations in which uniforms are required. See if your child notices people wearing uniforms. What is a uniform? Does each person's uniform have to be identical, or can they just have matching colors?

- The hospital bed in the story has a crank. Explain how this crank was used to make the bed "sit up." Today, many hospitals have beds that operate electronically.

- Sometimes the crack in the ceiling in the story looked like a rabbit. Lie on the floor with your child and look at the ceiling. Do you see anything that looks like something? Try different rooms with different patterns on the ceiling.

- Madeline goes to the hospital in an ambulance. Talk about what an ambulance does and why it's needed. Point out ambulances you see. If you're driving and hear a siren, explain the importance of getting out of the way so the ambulance can get to the hospital quickly.

- When the doctor calls the hospital, he dials "DANton-ten-six-." This phone number uses letters and numbers. Explain that today most people just use numbers. Then see if your child can say your phone number. Practice it together.

- You may enjoy watching the video **Madeline's Rescue** (CINAR Films, 1991).

Related Reading

Andrews, Jan. **Very Last First Time.** Macmillan, 1986.

Babbit, Natalie. **Phoebe's Revolt.** Farrar, 1988.

Bemelmans, Ludwig. **Madeline and the Bad Hat.** Viking, 1957.

Bemelmans, Ludwig. **Madeline in London.** Viking, 1961.

Bemelmans, Ludwig. **Madeline's Rescue.** Viking, 1953.

Gerrard, Jean. **Matilda Jane.** Farrar, 1983.

Jordan, June. **Kimako's Story.** Houghton, 1991.

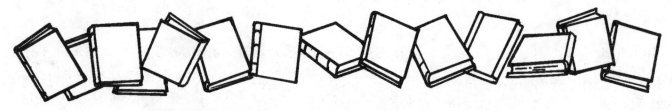

Make Way for Ducklings

Written and Illustrated by Robert McCloskey

Viking Press, 1941, 1961

Summary

One of the first and most famous Caldecott Medal winners concerns a family of Mallard ducks. Mr. and Mrs. Mallard decide that a small island in the Charles River of Boston is the perfect place to start a family. After the birth of eight ducklings, Mr. Mallard wants to move to the lake of the Public Garden. Mrs. Mallard teaches the ducklings to swim and walk in a line. They make their way across the city to meet Mr. Mallard at the pond. Crossing the busy streets is a problem until the city police come to the rescue. The family is reunited at the pond where there are many people who provide an endless supply of peanuts.

Hints for Reading Aloud

Be sure to make quacking noises. Your child will soon follow suit, and you can leave that job to him or her. Don't forget the honking of the cars and the tweeting of the policeman's whistle. You might want to add a few waddles and peeps.

What to Talk About

- The famous pictures in this story should provide hours of discussion for you and your child. Point out all the different buildings. Ask your child what kinds of people might live in them. The park pictures are full of bridges, benches, trees, and other plant life. Find out what your youngster has to say about all of these. Before long, this could become a favorite book for both of you. No doubt your child will be able to tell the entire story, providing his or her own ideas about how the ducks live in the park, what the policemen do when they are not looking after ducks, and what the people are thinking when Mrs. Mallard and the eight ducklings walk past.

Ideas and Activities

- Most city parks have ducks living there. Usually mid-morning and late afternoon will find them parading along the shore of a pond. Your child will love seeing them. But be warned—you'll probably be asked to read **Make Way for Ducklings** as soon as you return home!

- At the library, find a book with pictures of different types of ducks. Have your child find the one which looks most like Mr. and Mrs. Mallard.

- In Boston Common in Massachusetts, there is a statue dedicated to **Make Way for Ducklings.** Find a picture of it and share it with your child.

- You might also locate some photographs of American cities in the early 1940s. Look for similar buildings, cars, street lights, and park scenes that are shown in the story. How are the photos different from your child's perception of modern city life?

- This book provides an excellent opportunity to review safety rules for crossing the street. Remind children that they should always cross at a light, a crosswalk, or a corner. Talk about looking both ways and holding an adult's hand. Stress the importance of never running out from between parked cars to cross a street.

- Ducks are birds that swim. Find out about other types of birds that swim as well as fly. What are some types of birds that do not swim? What are some types of birds that do not fly?

Related Reading

Ellis, Anne Leo. **Dabble Duck.** Harper, 1984.

Farber, Norma. **As I Was Crossing Boston Common.** Dutton, 1991.

Friskey, Margaret. **Seven Diving Ducks.** Childrens, 1965.

Ichikawa, Satomi. **Nora's Duck.** Putnam, 1991.

Lyon, David. **The Runaway Duck.** Lothrop, 1985.

McCloskey, Robert. **Blueberries for Sal.** Viking, 1948.

McCloskey, Robert. **One Morning in Maine.** Viking, 1952.

Otto, Carolyn. **Ducks, Ducks, Ducks.** Harper, 1991.

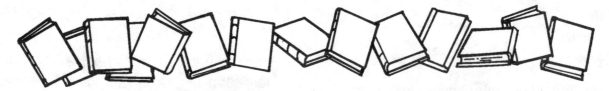

Mama, Do You Love Me?

Written by Barbara M. Joosse

Illustrated by Barbara Lavallee

Chronicle Books, 1991

Summary

In this beautifully illustrated book, a little Inuit girl asks her mother the age old childhood question, "Mama, do you love me?" The little girl begins to question her mother as to how much. The mother replies by using various animals and items from the Inuit culture to reassure her daughter that even if she became a polar bear and scared her own mother, she would still love her child dearly. This wonderfully comforting book gives the reader a glimpse into the richness of the Inuit culture.

Hints for Reading Aloud

This book is filled with questions that the little girl poses almost as a challenge to her mother. As you read the part of the little girl, make her voice innocent but insistent. When she asks about turning into bigger animals, such as a musk-ox, make her sound a bit incredulous. When you say the mother's part, read it with comforting assurance that comes when a parent needs to reassure a child about her mother's love for her.

What to Talk About

- Ask about some of the animals that your child might want to turn into if she or he were the child in the story.
- Talk to your youngster about love. What is it that makes people love each other?
- In the story, the mother constantly reassures her daughter that no matter what happens, she will always love her. This might be a good time to talk about loving your child at all times, even when she or he makes poor choices.

Ideas and Activities

- Before reading, preview the last few pages. They have excellent background information about the Inuit, the artifacts, and the animals mentioned in the story.

- The little girl and her mother are Inuit. Sometimes these people are referred to as Eskimos. On a world map, show that they live in the Arctic near the North Pole. Then point to where you live. How far is the Arctic from your home?

- Many animals native to the Arctic are mentioned in the book. Find out more about creatures such as the ermine, lemming, musk-ox, polar bear, ptarmigan, and puffin, by reading in an encyclopedia or other nonfiction book.

- The pictures show how people lived long ago. Which things, such as clothing, toys, and vehicles, can still be seen today?

- With your child make a card or write a poem for someone you love. On the cover, you might begin with the phrase, "Do you know how much I love you?" Then use words or pictures on the inside. A young child can dictate the text to you as you write it. You can work together to decorate the card and deliver it.

- Learn to say "I love you" in different languages. For example, in French it is "je t'aime," while in Spanish one would say "yo te amo." Try saying these to one another.

- The Inuit live in an extremely cold climate. Talk about cold weather and how to stay warm. What did the little girl and her mother wear for warmth? What would you wear? Gather those items. Compare them to the ones shown in the book.

- With your child, write your own version of this book. You might begin with "Daddy, Do You Love Me?" Then tell your own story of ways to show your love. Use crayons or markers for the illustrations. Have the author and illustrator sign it. Then write the date it was created so you can cherish it as a keepsake.

Related Reading

Alexander, Bryan and Cherry. **An Eskimo Family.** Lerner, 1985.

Alexander, Bryan and Cherry. **Inuit.** Raintree, 1993.

Fluornoy, Valerie. **The Patchwork Quilt.** Dial, 1985.

Gackenbach, Dick. **With Love From Gran.** Houghton, 1989.

Greenfield, Eloise. **Grandmama's Joy.** Putnam, 1980.

Hazen, Barbara S. **Even If I Did Something Awful?** Macmillan, 1992.

Hines, Anna Grossnickle. **It's Just Me, Emily.** Houghton, 1987.

Lindberg, Reeve. **Grandfather's Lovesong.** Viking, 1993.

Osinski, Alice. **The Eskimo: The Inuit and Yupik Peoples.** Childrens Press, 1985.

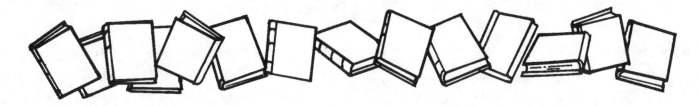

Millions of Cats

Written and Illustrated by Wanda Gag

Coward-McCann, Inc., 1928, 1977

Summary

One of the first "picture books" by an American artist has a fanciful, fairy tale look. An old man sees that his wife looks sad and realizes that they are lonely. He decides to get a cat. She asks for "a sweet little fluffy cat." He sets out over the hills and finds a land "covered with cats." He picks out one, then two, then three, but it is difficult to pick just one out of "billions and billions." So he takes them all. On the way home, they drink an entire pond and eat all the grass from the hills. Back at the couple's house, the wife is overwhelmed and not quite sure what to do. Then the old man has an idea. He asks which one is the prettiest cat. Each of them thinks it is. There is such squabbling that they end up eating each other. However, there is one scraggly one left. This kitten knew she was not the prettiest, so she didn't say anything and was not bothered by the other cats. The man and his wife take it home, feed it, and comb it. Soon it is indeed a pretty cat and just what the old woman wanted in the first place.

Hints for Reading Aloud

As you read the dialogue for the old man and woman, make your voice sound old by slowing down the pace and forcing a scratchy sound. Create a special sound for the cats when they say they are hungry and thirsty. Give the last little kitten a frightened, soft sound.

What to Talk About

- Ask where your child thinks so many cats might live. Find out what he or she thinks cats are like. If you have a cat, ask your child if it is like the kitten which was left. If you don't have a cat, ask how they are different from other animals that are more familiar to your child. Discuss why the old man felt he had to take all the cats when the old woman only wanted one.

Ideas and Activities

- Go to the library with your child and find a book about cat breeds. Examine their differences. While there, get a book about large cats, such as tigers, and show how they resemble ordinary house cats. Check out one of the books your child especially enjoys. Ask if he or she would like to draw one or more of the cats in the book.

- If you are thinking about getting a kitten or other pet, make your child part of this experience. There are many books written for children about proper pet care. Your child should be aware of the responsibilities as well as the fun of having a pet. Make it clear to your child that a pet is a living animal and must be treated with respect as well as love.

- The story is about millions of cats. How much is a million? With your child, think of things that come in millions. Can you visualize millions of cats? Write out the figure for one million (1,000,000). How many digits does it have? How about a billion and a trillion?

- This story is illustrated in black and white using pen and ink. Let your child draw a black and white cat. With young children, have them use black and white crayons or markers on white paper. With older children, you might try pen and ink to see if they can replicate some of the author-illustrator's unique style.

- **Millions of Cats** was published in 1928. This book has endured as a favorite through the years. With your child, think about the differences between your home and the homes of children who read or heard the story when it was first published. For instance, in 1928 there were no televisions or telephone answering machines.

Related Reading

Dubanevick, Arlene. **Tom's Tail.** Viking, 1990.

Formen, Michael. **Cat and Canary.** Macmillan, 1968.

Gantos, Jack. **Rotten Ralph.** Houghton, 1976.

Haley, Gail E., Reteller. **Puss in Boots.** Dutton, 1991.

Hofsepian, Sylvia. **Why Not?** Macmillan, 1991.

Ross, Tony. **I Want a Cat.** Farrar, 1989.

Schwartz, David. **If You Made a Million.** Lothrop, 1989.

Titus, Eve. **The Kitten Who Couldn't Purr.** Morrow, 1991.

The Mitten

Retold by Alvin Tresselt

Illustrated by Yaroslava Mills

Lothrop, Lee and Shepard 1989

Summary

In this retelling of an old Ukrainian folk tale, a little boy gathering wood for his grandmother on the coldest day of the year loses a mitten. Unaware that he no longer has the mitten, he begins his trek home. A freezing little mouse happens upon the mitten and crawls into it to keep warm. She is soon joined by animals that are progressively bigger, including a bear! When, at last, a tiny cricket joins the crowd, the mitten splits, dispersing the animals just before the boy comes back to find only a trace of his mitten.

Hints for Reading Aloud

When reading this story, keep giving the impression that the mitten is getting more and more full. Each character can have its own voice, from the little mouse to the huge bear who insists there is enough room for him. As the mitten falls apart with a rip and snap, give the words the sounds that they make.

What to Talk About

- Would all the animals truly have fit into the mitten?

- Why was the cricket the one to finally split the mitten? Was it really her fault?

- How would you describe the animals? Was it surprising to see animals that normally wouldn't get along, such as a wolf and a mouse, sharing the mitten?

- What lessons can be learned from all the animals sharing the close quarters that the mitten had to offer them?

Ideas and Activities

- Trace your hand and your child's on a piece of construction paper to form a mitten shape. Cut the patterns out and decorate them. Compare the sizes of your hands.

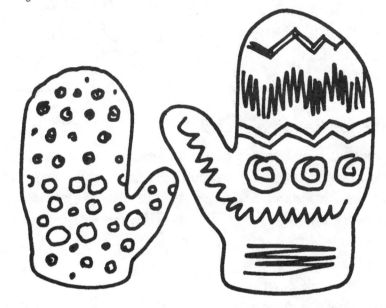

- Find a pair of knitted mittens that you no longer need. Decide on some objects that might fit into them. Guess how many objects will fit into one of the mittens before falling out. With your child, place the items one by one into the mitten. How close were you?

- Read another version of the story. How are they alike, and how are they different?

- This is a story that builds upon itself. Read **The Napping House** by Audrey Wood and determine how these two stories are alike. Old songs such as "This Is the House That Jack Built" or "There Was an Old Lady Who Swallowed a Fly" are also examples of this. These are fun and your child will enjoy hearing the words over and over again.

- It is the coldest day of the year when the mitten is lost. The animals crawl in to keep warm. Talk to your child about very cold weather and how to keep warm. Do you need caps and mittens? What else might you need? If you live where it gets really cold, this would be a good opportunity to check the cold weather clothing you have for both you and your child. Make a list of what you will need to get.

- Play some mitten matching games. If mittens are not available, then use socks. Place several mittens in a sack. Empty the sack, and see how quickly your child can match the pairs of mittens together. You can add some fun to this by placing the empty sack several feet away and having your child run and put the mittens in the sack. Remember that a young child may only be able to match one or two pairs of mittens. If the task seems too hard for your child, you probably have too many mittens in the bag.

Related Reading

Brett, Jan (Reteller) **The Mitten.** Putnam, 1990.

Glazer, Tom. **Tom Glazer's Treasury of Songs for Children.** Doubleday, 1964.

Rylant, Cynthia. **The Relatives Came.** Macmillan, 1985.

Wood, Audrey. **The Napping House.** Harcourt Brace, 1984.

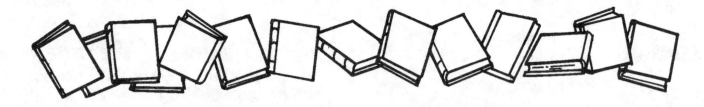

Mrs. Katz and Tush

Written and Illustrated by Patricia Polacco

A Bantam Little Rooster Book, 1992

Summary

Larnel, a young African-American boy, develops a long-lasting friendship with Mrs. Katz, an elderly Jewish widow. Larnel brings Mrs. Katz a small cat which relieves her loneliness. Mrs. Katz relives her memories by telling Larnel about her life. Larnel learns how much the two cultures have in common. In one incident, the cat, Tush, gets lost, and Larnel's father finds it cold and starving in an alley. Mrs. Katz becomes a part of Larnel's family. As Larnel grows into manhood, he remembers Mrs. Katz.

Hints for Reading Aloud

Mrs. Katz should sound old. Make her speech slow and halting since English is not her first language. Make her sound very worried when Tush is lost. Larnel should sound very brave and sure of himself when he reassures Mrs. Katz, "I'll find her . . . I won't let you down!"

What to Talk About

- This is a good story to use to discuss relationships with your child. Talk about your parents and how their lives are different from your child's.

- If you have elderly people living in your neighborhood, ask your child about what special needs they may have.

- For older children, discuss similarities between your culture and others.

- What holidays do most people celebrate? What are some holidays that are special for only certain culture groups?

Ideas and Activities

- Have your child visit or call his or her grandparents and tell them about this story. If possible, let a grandparent read the story to your child. If a grandparent is not available, then visit with a senior citizen and ask this person to read the story to your child.

- Visit a local nursing home and talk to some of the residents. Ask your child if any of these people seem like Mrs. Katz.

- Some agencies provide animals for elderly people as company. Find out about this.

- Talk to elderly people on your street. Children will become more comfortable around older people if they get to know them.

- Make a list of words that different cultures use for grandmother. In the story, Mrs. Katz is called a bubbe, which is a Yiddish word. Does your child have a special name for his or her grandmother? Have your child ask some friends what they call their grandmothers.

- Mrs. Katz has a Passover seder to which Larnel is invited. Find out more about this celebration which helps commemorate the Jewish journey across the desert for freedom from Egyptian rule during Biblical times. The holiday is celebrated in the spring. Matzoh is mentioned in the story. It is often available in grocery stores around that time of year. You and your child might enjoy trying this cracker-type bread.

- Mrs. Katz comes from the "old country." For her, this is Warsaw, Poland. Also mentioned are the Catskills, mountains located in New York. Show the two places to your child on a world map and estimate how far Mrs. Katz had to travel.

- Choose some music that you and your child both enjoy. Dress up in a costume and dance as Larnel and Mrs. Katz do.

Related Reading

dePaola, Tomie. **My First Passover.** Putnam, 1991.

Johnston, Tony. **The Promise.** Harper, 1992.

Peretz, I. L. **The Magician's Visit: A Passover Tale.** (Retold by Barbara D. Godin) Viking, 1993.

Polacco, Patricia. **The Bee Tree.** Putnam, 1993.

Zolotow, Charlotte. **I Know a Lady.** Greenwillow, 1984.

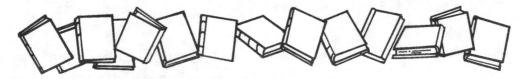

My Kwanzaa Story

Written by Bobbie Ballard

Illustrated by Charles Slay

Ujamaa Enterprises, 1993

Summary

Washeed is very excited as he eagerly anticipates the last night of Kwanzaa that he will soon celebrate with his family and friends. In this engaging story, the African-American cultural celebration of Kwanzaa is explained. Through the character Washeed, we see the significance of this relatively new holiday unfold. The seven principles, the "nguzo saba," are fully explained as is the significance of each of the symbols.

Hints for Reading Aloud

As many of the words that relate to Kwanzaa are from the Swahili language, you may need to practice them before you say them. This book helps to simplify this task by giving the word and a phonetic pronunciation guide. Make sure, in your reading of the phonetic reading, that you give the emphasis to the letters that appear in capitals. Washeed is very excited about this celebration. Let your voice show the excitement when you read Washeed's explanations about the holiday. You will want to share the pictures in this book so your child can see what the story is explaining.

What to Talk About

- Talk to your child about the significance of this holiday. The principles of Kwanzaa are ones that everyone can live by. You may want to read these again with your child.

- Together, choose one of the principles and expand on it. Ask how that principle could best be demonstrated in daily life. Share what you would do to practice one of the principles.

Ideas and Activities

- There are many foods associated with Kwanzaa. Corn is representative of the children in a family. Cook an ear of corn for each child in your family. Enjoy sharing the corn.

- The guests dance to the beat of the African-American rhythm. Find some music with songs that would have a similar beat. Play the music and dance to it.

- The story explains that the colors of the lit candles have a special meaning. Find out how colors can have other meanings in different situations. This is often true in flags of various nations.

- Kwanzaa is a time when the past is thought about and remembered. With your child, take time to remember the past. Very young children do not have a lot to remember, but it might be a good time to talk about your family history or tell favorite family stories. Photographs are always a good way to get a family discussion started, so share some if you have them.

- During Kwanzaa, African Americans celebrate a time of thanksgiving. With your child, think of things you are thankful for. Make a list to remind yourself when you or your child feel downhearted. In addition, find out about the other holidays or celebrations during which people give thanks. These include the American Thanksgiving, the Canadian Thanksgiving, and the Jewish Succoth.

- With your child, make a list of famous African-American heroes. Examples include Jackie Robinson, Rosa Parks, Dr. Martin Luther King, Jr., and Mary McLeod Bethune. Read some books to learn more about these people and their deeds.

Related Reading

Burden-Patman, Denise. **Imani's Gift of Kwanzaa.** Simon & Schuster, 1993.

Chocolate, Deborah M. **Kwanzaa.** Childrens Press, 1990.

Chocolate, Deborah M. **My First Kwanzaa.** Scholastic, 1992.

Freeman, Dorothy R. and Diane M. **Kwanzaa.** (Illustration Series: **Best Holiday Books**) Enslow, 1992.

Porter, A. P. **Kwanzaa.** Carolrhoda, 1991.

Walter, Mildred P. **Have a Happy...** Lothrop, Lee and Shepard, 1989.

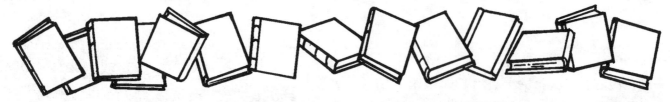

Never Spit on Your Shoes

Written and Illustrated by Denys Cazet
Orchard Books, 1990

Summary

Arnie comes home from his first day of first grade to a plate of cookies and a mother who is anxious to hear about his adventures. As Arnie tells his mother about the trials and tribulations of first grade, including no naps and learning how to spell "boys", she eats lots of cookies. As we learn early on, one of the rules in first grade is to "Never spit on your shoes." The major text is set into boxes, while the rest of the page provides for a comical look at what is really going on in the first grade.

Hints for Reading Aloud

The story is a dialogue between Arnie and his mother. As he tells the story, she listens. When Arnie is telling his mother about his day, make your voice sound young and tired. Arnie's mother wants to get more information from him than he is willing to tell. Let her voice be a bit wary of what Arnie is saying.

Since the pages of this book are filled with the delightful goings-on in first grade, share the pictures and the secondary text with your child after reading the major text. You may want to give the characters voices, or you may want to read what's on the chalkboard.

What to Talk About

- This is a great book to read just before school begins, especially for a child about to enter the first grade. Discuss any fears your child has about beginning school. What do you think will be different from last year? What do you expect to learn this year? What rules would you make for your class? Why do you think those rules are important?

Ideas and Activities

- Arnie learns how to spell b-o-y-s very quickly. Ask your child why that is important and then decide what other words might be important to be able to read and spell at school. This might include your child's name, as well as the words boys, girls, principal, and office. Make a list of these words and practice spelling and reading them.

- Arnie helps Raymond count to 16. He helps him by using his toes. With your child, see how high you can count. Then associate numbers to objects by counting something like pennies or paper clips.

- For the first time, Arnie eats lunch in the school cafeteria. Talk about the eating arrangements at school. Is there a cafeteria? Can you buy a lunch? If so, talk about what foods would be good for lunch. If your child will be taking a lunch, make a list of what to put in it. You might want to go to the store and get all the necessary things and practice packing a lunch well before school starts. Then you can always go to the park for a picnic.

- Give your child an opportunity to write on a chalkboard. Secure a small, old-fashioned slate and some chalk. Have your youngster draw a picture or write some words. Then erase the slate and start all over again.

- Read aloud a story about a giant. A good one is **Jack and the Beanstalk.**

- The illustrations in this story make the unwritten story as full as the written one. Have your child look at the surrounding pictures. Invite your child to create his or her own stories, about the first grade, using those pictures.

- The rule, "Never spit on your shoes," is a humorous one. With your child, make up other funny rules that might make sense to follow in school or at home.

Related Reading

Ashley, Bernard. **Cleversticks.** Crown, 1991.

Cazet, Denys. **Frosted Glass.** Macmillan, 1987.

Cazet, Denys. **Good Morning, Maxine.** Macmillan, 1989.

Cohen, Miriam. **First Grade Takes a Test.** Dell, 1983.

Howe, James. **The Day the Teacher Went Bananas.** Dutton, 1984.

Lawlor, Laurie. **Second Grade Dog.** Whitman, 1990.

Stevenson, James. **That Dreadful Day.** Greenwillow, 1985.

Weiss, Leatie. **My Teacher Sleeps in School.** Puffin, 1985.

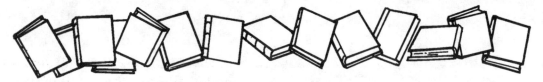

Ox-Cart Man

Written by Donald Hall

Illustrated by Barbara Cooney

Puffin Books, 1983

Summary

A colonial family works hard all year on their farm. In October, the father gathers everything left over that the family has not used to live on and puts it into his ox-cart. Then he walks ten days into Portsmouth. At Portsmouth Market, he sells everything, including apples, maple sugar, goose feathers, candles, and wool. He even sells the ox-cart and the ox. He buys a few items that the family will need for the next year and splurges on two pounds of peppermint candies. He puts his purchases inside a new kettle and walks back home. His family greets him and starts to work again, making and growing everything the family will need for the upcoming year.

Hints for Reading Aloud

There is no dialogue in this simple but beautiful book. Take your time reading the story. Allow time for your child to listen to the words and carefully study the illustrations. Emphasize the lines that show what the children have contributed to the family.

What to Talk About

• Point out elements in the illustrations. Have your child notice the fall landscape and the change of seasons on the last pages. Call attention to the colors of the sky and the cloud formations. Point out the different items made and grown by the family as you read about them.

Ask your child some or all of the following questions:

• Is the family happy? How can you tell?
• Does the farmer mind his ten-day walk to the market?
• Does he feel sad about selling the ox? Why or why not?
• What is one thing the farmer buys that the family cannot use to help themselves on the farm? Why do you think he buys this?

Ideas and Activities

- Children who live in cities and towns are usually fascinated by farm life. Have your child talk about this. If you know someone who owns a farm, visit it. If you have a flower or vegetable garden, allow your child to help plant, water, weed, and harvest it. Otherwise, help your child plant something in an indoor pot. You will probably be surprised at how much your child enjoys watching things grow.

- If you do not live in a farming community, take a drive out into farm country and point out vistas that remind you of those in the book.

- Older children might find nonfictional accounts of Colonial family life interesting. Some suggestions can be found in the **Related Reading**.

- In the book, the family makes things that they need. With your child, name items that you could make. For an enjoyable project, create a simple item that you might not normally make, such as a pillow.

- In the story, we see the year go through its cycle. Talk about the four seasons with your child. Make a seasons chart to keep track of the changing weather. To do this, simply fold or draw four squares on a large sheet of paper or take four sheets of paper and label them **Summer, Fall, Winter,** and **Spring.** Then choose an appropriate symbol for each type of weather. Every day during a particular season, draw the symbol that represents the type of weather you had. Weather stickers can be used instead of drawings. With a young child, place weather stickers on the chart only every so often. See if the types of stickers you use change as the seasons change. Do you wear different clothing? Do you play outdoors longer?

- The children get a gift of peppermints from their father. What makes this such a special treat? Taste some peppermints with your child, and decide if this would be something special today.

Related Reading

Bartone, Elisa. **Peppe the Lamplighter.** Lothrop, 1993.

Benchley, Nathaniel. **George the Drummer Boy.** Harper, 1977.

Brown, Ruth. **The World That Jack Built.** Dutton, 1991.

Castaneda, Omar S. **Abuela's Weave.** Lee, 1993.

McPhail, David. **Farm Boy's Year.** Macmillan, 1992.

Pryof, Bonnie. **The House on Maple Street.** Morrow, 1992.

Waters, Kate. **Sara Morton's Day: A Day in the Life of a Pilgrim Girl.** Scholastic, 1989.

Peek-A-Boo!

Written and Illustrated by Janet and Allan Ahlberg

Puffin Books, 1981

Summary

This book contains several cut-out circles. Through each one, a baby looks into his world. Each illustration is from the baby's perspective as he sees his family going through its daily routine. This particular family lives in England during World War II. The story's clever rhyme and wonderful pictures will delight your child.

Hints for Reading Aloud

The rhymes in this book make it particularly easy to read. At the end of each rhyme, on the next page, you will find the words "PEEK-A-BOO!" under the cutout. Each time you come to these exclamations, read them with gusto as the capitals and exclamation points indicate. Depending on how many times you have read this book, you may want to stop and let your child describe what she or he sees. Then turn the page and with your child read what the baby sees.

What to Talk About

- The story lends itself to discussion for every page since each ends with "What does he see?" You can ask your child that question as many times as you read this book and still not have all the answers. You can ask the question as a precursor to the next page, or you can read the answers. Another way to enjoy this book is to let your child look at the picture with you and name as many things as possible that are in it.

- Talk about the family. How is it like yours? How is it different?

Ideas and Activities

- The story takes place in England during World War II. Explain the times very simply to your child. Then explain that the father in the story goes off at night to work in order to help the war effort.

- Some of the words may not be familiar to your child. See if using context clues and reading the story several times helps clarify these words. Ask your child what a flannel (washcloth) might be or what grandma is doing when she is pegging washing (hanging it up to dry). Together decide on some words that only your family might say or write that other people wouldn't understand unless they were used in context.

- The baby's night clothes are warmed on the oven door. Talk about why this wouldn't be very safe but that during the war it might have been the only way to stay warm. How could this be done safely today? Could the baby's things be put in a clothes dryer for a few minutes?

- Mother, Father, and Baby all look in the mirror together. Have some fun making faces in a mirror with your child.

- Play Peek-a-Boo. This can be accomplished with a handkerchief, cloth, or hand that is held up over your eyes. Depending on your child's age, you may need to be the one who hides. **Note:** Many children get frightened if they hide their eyes. Just hold the cloth or hand in front of your face and call "Peek-a-Boo!"

- Make a peek-a-boo card. The cutouts in this book allow a child to focus on just a small section of a very busy page. Use an index card and cut out a circle from the middle of it. Place the card on the page with the circle over an object in a picture. Ask your child what he or she sees. This activity can be done with any book.

- Play a version of I Spy, using the pictures in the book. These pictures are rich in detail. Choose an object in one picture and describe it. Start with one small detail as your clue and ask your child to guess what the object is. Keep adding details until your youngster names the object.

Related Reading

Ahlberg, Janet and Allan. **The Jolly Postman (or Other People's Letters)**. Little, Brown and Company, 1986.

Aruegueo, Jose, and Arian Dewey. **We Hide, You Seek.** Morrow, 1979.

Livermore, Elaine. **Find the Cat.** Houghton, 1973.

Shaw, Charles. **It Looked Like Spilt Milk.** Harper, 1947.

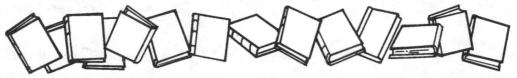

Q Is for Duck: An Alphabet Guessing Game

Written by Mary Elting and Michael Folsom

Illustrated by Jack Kent

Houghton Mifflin, 1980

Summary

The subtitle, **An Alphabet Guessing Game**, sums up the concept of this book which encourages critical thinking involving the alphabet. Each letter of the alphabet is given a question as to what the letter stands for. The letters do not take the typical "A is for apple" route. Rather they use association with something that goes along with what the items do. For instance, in this book G is for horse. Why, you might ask, would G stand for horse when it usually stands for goat? The answer is quite simple. "G is for horse because a horse gallops."

Children who already know the alphabet will find this book highly amusing. However, it may confuse those who are just learning letter sounds and word associations. Be selective in your reading.

Hints for Reading Aloud

Each letter begins with a statement that tells what the letter stands for. After the statement comes the question "Why?" Each time you read "Why?" stop and let your child guess why the letter stands for that particular item.

After a few readings of this book, your child will know all the whys, but that will add to the fun. When you read the answers to the questions, the key words, what the letter stands for is written in a large colored capital letter. Let your voice reflect the largeness by using a big voice when you read words such as "Cluck" or "Roars."

On some pages, there is text as part of the illustration. When appropriate, include that in your reading. Also, act out any of the movements that might be mentioned, such as scratching for the mosquito.

What to Talk About

- Ask your child to say the ABC's. Then ask for some examples of what he or she thinks each letter stands for.

- After reading the story, ask why the letters stand for the things that they do. Help your child with the concept.

Ideas and Activities

- Make up your own Alphabet Guessing Game. Choose some letters and decide what they stand for. Use an index card and write a letter and a statement on the front. Then write the question, "Why?" Example: B is for cute. Why? On the back of the card, write the answer. Example: Because babies are cute. Play the game with your child, taking turns guessing what each letter stands for.

- Read other alphabet books. There are so many to choose from that you might be able to find one that matches a special interest that your child has, such as dinosaurs or bugs. Some suggestions are given in the **Related Reading**.

- Make an alphabet collage. Let your child glue pictures torn from magazines onto a large sheet of paper. Help write the first letter of each picture name.

- Notice that in the book all the letters are represented by some type of animal. With your child, create an animal alphabet. Be on the lookout for animals that might fit the letters X and U. You might not include these at the beginning of the word so that foX can stand for X.

- In the book the mule kicks and the frog leaps. Find other actions and motions performed by the animals. Perform these actions with your child. Pantomime an action while your child guesses the animal.

- Visit a zoo. By watching the live animals, see if you can determine why the author made the particular association with the animal in the book.

- Help your child recognize the first letter in his or her first name. Children are very possessive of their first initials and often learn to recognize and write them long before they learn any other letters.

- Obtain some computer software that gives your child the opportunity to learn the alphabet. Suggestion: **Curious George: ABC Adventure** by Houghton Mifflin Interactive. CD-ROM for MAC and PC. Available from Educorp, 7434 Trade Street, San Diego, CA 92121-2410. 1-800-843-9497.

Related Reading

Anno, Misumasa. **Anno's Alphabet: An Adventure in Imagination.** Harper, 1975.

Pollata, Jerry. **The Frog Alphabet Book...and Other Awesome Amphibians.** Charlesbridge, 1990.

Van Allsburg, Chris. **The Z Was Zapped: A Play in Twenty-Six Acts.** Houghton, 1987.

Watson, Clyde. **Applebet: An ABC.** Farrar, 1982.

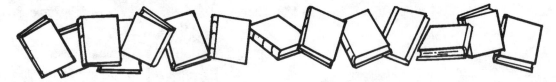

Rainbow Crow

Retold by Nancy Van Laan

Illustrated by Beatriz Vidal

Alfred A. Knopf, 1989

Summary

This Native American fable begins when snow comes for the first time to Earth. The animals are curious. However, they become frightened when it begins to cover them. Because the animals cannot agree on which one of them should confront the Sky Spirit, the rainbow crow volunteers. He is given fire by the Spirit. As he flies, black soot from the flame covers his colorful feathers and clogs his throat, ruining his beautiful voice. The crow is forever changed by his brave act. However, the Sky Spirit tells the crow it will forever remain the only free animal when the humans become master over the Earth.

Hints for Reading Aloud

The crow never speaks in the book; he only sings. Your child might enjoy hearing you sing the crow's song. You can make up a simple tune. The sad loss of the crow's voice would be all the more apparent if its song is sung. Although the "caw" of the crow is not used, you might add it toward the end as it sadly sits on the branch of the tree. The Sky Spirit's voice could be deep and full of authority. The larger animals might sound booming while the smaller animals sound soft and low.

As you read, let your child know this is a Native American fable. Point out that a fable is meant to explain certain occurrences in nature. After hearing the book a few times, your child might be able to sing or chant some of the songs. Invite your child to help you "read" the story. The words do not have to be exactly what is written in the book.

What to Talk About

- Discuss how the rainbow crow shows bravery. An older child may want to talk about the different ways a person can be brave. Remember to explain that in order for people to be courageous, they must be willing to risk losing something they consider very important. Discuss what the crow loses.

- Talk about why the other animals could not decide who should talk to the Sky Spirit. Why is the crow a good choice? Does the fact that the crow can fly make it the best choice to visit the Spirit?

Ideas and Activities

- Your library may have Native American stories and fables from other cultures your child would enjoy. Share any of Aesop's fables that you remember. One day your child may study mythology. This is a fine way to make an early connection.

- **Rainbow Crow** is a legend from the Lenape tribe who lived in the Eastern Woodlands in Eastern Pennsylvania. These people traveled by foot and canoe and ate mostly what they could trap or hunt. Find the area on a map of the United States. Show it to your child. How far were the Lenape from where you live?

- Create a brightly colored rainbow crow based on one of the illustrations. If your child has never tried watercolors, you may wish to buy a set. The pictures will take on a new dimension which crayons or colored pencils can't duplicate.

- Make a color book with your child. Staple a number of blank sheets together. Write the names of six to eight colors, one per page. The color of each word should match the name of the color. Have your child draw items on each page that have that color. On the "red" page, there might be a wagon, a firetruck, and an apple. If your child sees the brown dog next door as red, use it as a time to discuss how colors may appear different to people. You can also find color pictures in magazines to cut and glue into your child's book.

- Obtain a software version of a Native American folk tale such as **Sleeping Cub's Test of Courage** by Kudos. CD-ROM for MAC and WIN. Available from Davidson & Assoc., P.O. Box 2961, Torrance, CA 90503. 1-800-545-7677.

Related Reading

Aesop. **An Aesop Fable: The Tortoise and the Hare.** Holiday, 1984.

Ash, Russell, and Bernard A. Higton, eds. **Aesop's Fables.** Chronicle, 1991.

Baylor, Byrd. **And It Is Still That Way: Legends Told by Arizona Indian Children.** Trails West Paper, 1987.

Bierhorst, John. **The Woman Who Fell From the Sky: The Iroquois Story of Creation.** Morrow, 1993.

Connolly, James E. **Why the Possum's Tail Is Bare: And Other North American Indian Nature Tales.** Stemmer, 1993.

Mayo, Gretchen Will. **Star Tales: North American Indian Stories About the Stars.** Walker, 1987.

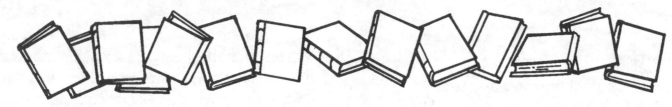

The Relatives Came

Written by Cynthia Rylant

Illustrated by Stephen Gammell

Bradbury Press, 1985

Summary

The relatives travel by car from Virginia. They pass many strange houses, but they finally arrive. There is endless hugging and crying. There are not enough beds, but everyone manages. The house becomes a different place with the relatives there. They stay many weeks and help out any way they can. They eat up all the fruit but promise that "we" can do the same when visiting them in Virginia. Then it comes time for the relatives to leave. The house is too quiet without them. Everyone thinks about seeing each other next summer.

Hints for Reading Aloud

There is no dialogue in this book. Emphasize the details that make this story special—"the bologna sandwiches, the box of crackers, the ice chest full of soda pop." The repetition of the "purple grapes" and the other fruits mentioned can also be stressed.

What to Talk About

• The appealing illustrations can spark endless discussions.

• Ask your child what makes these relatives special. Responses might include the way they help fix things, their musical instruments, the sleeping arrangements, and the way everyone is always smiling.

• If you live in the city, talk about how the people in this book live compared to your family. How would a reunion in a city house or apartment be different from the one in the book?

• Since there are so many various people in the illustrations, have your child try to find the same ones in different drawings. How can you tell they are the same people? By their clothing? expressions? size? Let your child tell you, and if he or she makes a good argument, don't disagree.

Ideas and Activities

- Think about the last visit you had from relatives. How was it similar to and different from the one in this book? Allow your child to have his or her own viewpoint. It might surprise you to learn how different your child's perception is from yours.

- Family relationships can be very confusing. Talk about how people in your family are related to one another. Don't expect your child to easily understand all the connections. Answer as many of your youngter's questions as you can.

- Your child might be confused about the difference between relatives and good friends. A child often wants to know whether a best friend is related since this person is probably seen much more often than uncles or aunts. Be patient and enjoy how your child is trying to work out the complications.

- Make a family tree with your child. This can be just two generations, or you can extend it back as far as you wish. Using a piece of paper, write your child's name and then draw a line up to each side for both parents. Write mom and dad's names. From here just keep adding any family members that you choose.

- The relatives helped to fix the house and work in the garden. Let your child help you do those things. If you can do some of it with extended family members, it will be more fun for your child.

- The relatives came from Virginia. Show Virginia to your child on a map of the United States. Show where you live and where some of your relatives live. Determine the best way to get to those relatives. Are they close enough to walk to, or would you need a car or plane to get there? How long would it take to get there?

Related Reading

Bond, Felicia. **Poinsettia and Her Family**. Harper, 1981.

Drescher, Joan. **Your Family, My Family.** Walker, 1980.

Miller, Edna. **Mousekin's Family**. Prentice, 1972.

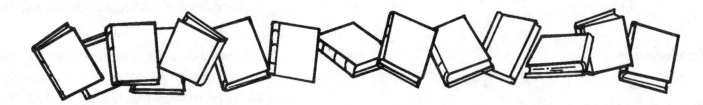

Richard Scarry's Cars and Trucks and Things That Go

Written and Illustrated by Richard Scarry

Western Publishing, 1974

Summary

The Pig family, Ma, Pa, Penny, and Pickles, are all going on a picnic. They have decided to go to the beach—but, oh, how to get there and what they will see! The Pigs make many stops along the way, having a grand adventure as part of their journey. They also see almost every conceivable type of transportation along the way. Trucks, trains, and trolleys fill this whimsical look at transportation.

Hints for Reading Aloud

The text for the story is written in a boldfaced print that you can find on each page. As you read the dialogue, look at what has happened to decide what kind of voice to use. Sometimes the Pig speaking is very excited and at other times, sad. However, don't be too surprised if you don't read much of the story. As you show your child the book, chances are he or she will only want to look at the pictures and have you tell (or tell you) about all the types of transportation shown on each page.

What to Talk About

- This book lends itself to talking about the many ways that people and objects get around. Choose any of the vehicles and ask your child what it does. What special functions might it perform? Where would one find such a vehicle? Would you like to drive one or ride in one? How fast do you think it might go?

Ideas and Activities

- There is a special little character called "Goldbug" found on many of the pages. With your child, search the pages until one of you finds it.

- The Pigs go to the gas station. Take your child to a gas station. Explain safety rules first. For a young child, just point out things. An older child can help wipe the windshield.

- Make a three-column chart labeled **Land, Sea,** and **Air,** and write the types of vehicles from the story on it. Which has the most? Ask what kinds of transportation your child has used. Remind her or him about past trips. Make a list that includes a bicycle, elevator, and red wagon. Add to it whenever you go out.

- Make sailboats using Ivory™ soap, scissors, index paper or cards, tape, and toothpicks. Cut a triangle out of the paper. Tape it onto the side of the toothpick. Press the toothpick into the soap. Put the soap boat into a basin of water and blow.

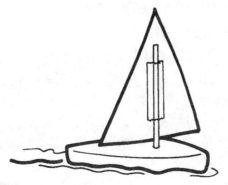

- Play cars together. Blocks make dandy roads and towns, and pillows are great mountains. Use chalk on a sidewalk to create a highway. Use this time to teach traffic safety. Look at a stoplight. Explain that red means stop, yellow means caution, and green means go. Explain what a stop sign means to a driver.

- Play the license plate game while driving. Have young children just find the licenses. Have older children tell when the licenses are from different states, or have them look for a certain letter or read the words on the plates.

- Visit an airport to watch the planes. Then have your child draw a picture of what he or she saw.

- Go to a harbor and try to find a sailboat, a motorboat, and a fishing boat. If you live near a lake and the ocean, visit both and compare the two.

- Use the following software: **Big Machines** by CounterTop. CD-ROM for MAC and PC. Available from Educorp, 7434 Trade St., San Diego, CA 92121-2410. 1-800-843-9497. As an alternative, watch the video **Mike Mulligan and His Steam Shovel** (Golden Book Video, 1992).

Related Reading

Borden, Louise. **The Neighborhood Trucker.** Scholastic, 1990.

Gramatky, Hardie. **Little Toot.** Putnam, 1939.

Hurd, Thatcher. **Axle the Freeway Cat.** Harper, 1981.

McPhail, David. **Ed and Me.** Harcourt, 1990.

Osbourne, Victor. **Rex, the Most Special Car in the World.** Carolrhoda, 1989.

School Days

Written by B.G. Hennessy

Illustrated by Tracey Campbell Peterson

Viking, 1990

Summary

Your preschooler through first grader will enjoy this typical day in a primary classroom. It is told in simple language with rhyming lines on succeeding pages. Beginning with a group of children entering the classroom, the story follows them through their learning, art projects, lunch, recess, and fire drill. The colorful pictures are full of moments that are common to all classrooms.

Hints for Reading Aloud

Emphasize the rhyme the first time through if your child lets you read it without interrupting and saying, "That looks like my classroom." Later, don't worry too much about it. Your child will pick up on the rhyme and help you finish the lines.

What to Talk About

- Your child will probably notice that the lines where the words are written resemble the primary writing paper used at school. If not, point it out. Have your child compare and contrast the pictures with his or her school. A child who is already reading may want to tell you certain words the author has used.

- If your child attends school, this book will provide an unending opportunity to compare his or her classroom with the one in the book. If your child is hesitant about discussing the school day, this book might provide the catalyst to open the lines of communication. However, don't force this. Your child will probably share information after seeing the book a few times.

- Look at the letters the illustrator puts over the chalkboard. Ask if they look like the ones in your child's classroom. This can be an excellent phonics lesson.

- Would your child agree that a couple of the children on the playground are being "very bad"? Judging from the clothes the children are wearing at recess, what season is it? If you live in a temperate climate, your child might not see these outer clothes at school at all.

Ideas and Activities

- Your child may enjoy writing some of the sentences from the story on primary writing paper.

- This might be a book your child wishes to share with friends at school. Suggest that your youngster show it to his or her teacher and ask if it could be read to the class.

- What goes into the children's lunches in the story? Compare them to the lunch your child eats each day. If it is very different from what your child takes, see if he or she would like to try some of the items mentioned in the book. Then, together, pack this lunch.

- Your child might see an activity in the illustrations that he or she would like to try with you at home. You might enjoy helping your child create the huge blue whale (on a smaller scale) or going to a jungle gym to see how he or she can also hang upside down.

- Examine the school picture. Count the children in it. Does your child's class have more or fewer students? Compare the number of boys and girls. See if your child can tell you the names of all the children in his or her class. Are any of the names the same as the ones in the book?

- Your child might want to share his or her own schedule at school. You can write it down together. Tell your child that you will keep it at home or take it to work so you can know what he or she is doing during the school day.

- Rent one of the many videos about school adventures such as **Arthur's Teacher Troubles** (Random House Home Video, 1997).

Related Reading

Burningham, John. **John Patrick Norman McHennessy— The Boy Who Was Always Late.** Crown, 1988.

Maurer, Donna. **Annie, Bea, and Chi Chi Dolores: A School Day Alphabet.** Orchard, 1993.

McMillan, Bruce. **Mouse View: What the Class Pet Saw.** Holiday, 1993.

Tyron, Leslie. **Albert's Alphabet.** Macmillan, 1991.

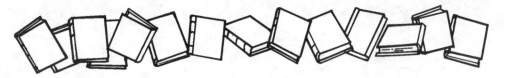

Song and Dance Man

Written by Karen Ackerman

Illustrated by Stephen Gammell

Alfred Knopf, 1988

Summary

Grandpa was a song and dance man during the days of vaudeville. Now, when his grandchildren come to visit, they all head up to the attic and Grandpa's old trunk. From his trunk he pulls out his hat, vest, cane, and tap shoes. He then puts on a rollicking show, singing, dancing, telling jokes, and even doing a magic trick or two. His grandchildren delight in his performance, calling for more, but Grandpa packs up his shoes and memories for another time and then delights in his grandchildren.

Hints for Reading Aloud

This story is a narrative with little dialogue. It is a lighthearted nostalgic look at Grandpa's days in vaudeville, so read it with a lighthearted tone. This is a good book for you to add some of your own sound effects. For instance, when the boxes and dresses are moved, add groaning sounds as if it is difficult. When Grandpa taps, you can make tapping sounds on a table. When the children laugh, laugh out loud. As the children call out "Hooray!" and "More!" say it numerous times, not just once as written. At the end of the story when Grandpa whispers, use a whisper. Pause before reading the last page, as if Grandpa is reflecting on his days in vaudeville.

What to Talk About

- The key to this story is understanding vaudeville. It was a type of entertainment in which people sang, danced, and told jokes, among other types of activities. It was live and on stage. Explain to your child that Grandpa in the story did this. If you have seen a live stage production, talk about it. How is it different from watching something on television or at the movies?

- Do you think Grandpa misses his vaudeville days?

- Would you have enjoyed watching him?

- What type of dancing do you like to do or watch?

Ideas and Activities

- Find out more about vaudeville. There are old movies on video that show some vaudeville scenes in them. **Singing in the Rain** begins with some scenes from a vaudeville show as does **Easter Parade.** These are often available at video stores. Watch them with your child to get a feel for times gone by.

- Dance with your child. Grandpa did tap dancing. This requires special shoes and steps, but you and your child can have fun just trying to tap. Who knows, you might even find that you will want to take lessons.

- Before television, people went to the theater to see vaudeville acts. They also amused themselves by playing games like checkers or cards or doing jigsaw puzzles. Turn your television off for an evening or more and find ways to amuse yourselves as in pretelevision times.

- Put on a show. This can be as simple as singing a song, reciting a verse, or telling a joke in front of an audience. With your child, decide what you want to do. The audience can be other siblings or neighborhood children. Get a light to serve as the spotlight; even a flashlight will do. Rehearse and then enjoy the talent.

- Learn a few magic tricks. If you live near a magic store, visit it and find out about some simple tricks your child can learn. Then perform them to amaze people.

- Grandpa sang "Yankee Doodle Boy." This is a song popularized by George M. Cohan. Find other patriotic songs and sing them.

- Let your child learn the elephant joke in the book. Then learn some more and tell them. Following are a couple to help get you started.

  What time is it when an elephant sits on your fence? Time to get a new fence.

  What's gray and has a trunk? An elephant going on vacation.

Related Reading

Alexander, Martha. **Where Does the Sky End, Grandpa?** Harcourt, 1992.

Blos, Joan W. **The Grandpa Days.** Simon & Schuster, 1989.

DeFelice, Cynthia. **When Grandpa Kissed His Elbow.** Macmillan, 1992.

Nodar, Carmen Santiago. **Abuelita's Paradise.** Whitman, 1992.

Porte, Barbara Ann. **When Grandma Almost Fell Off the Mountain and Other Stories.** Orchard, 1993.

Williams, Barbara. **Kevin's Grandma.** Puffin, 1991.

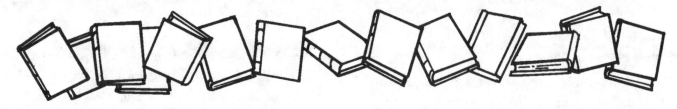

Stone Soup

Told and Illustrated by Marcia Brown

Aladdin, 1947, 1986

Summary

In this telling of **Stone Soup,** three hungry, tired soldiers arrive in a village. The townspeople are afraid they won't have enough to eat for themselves, so they hide their food from the soldiers. It is because of the soldiers' cleverness that they are able to get the whole village involved in making stone soup and creating a feast that is enjoyed by all.

Hints for Reading Aloud

Create the voices of each of the soldiers and the villagers. In the beginning, have the soldiers talk slowly and sound tired. When the soldiers tell the people about the stone soup, have them do it in a friendly fashion. As you read the book, let the story lead you along without ever giving away the naiveté of the people as they wonder over the making of stone soup.

What to Talk About

- The soldiers get their food at the end of the story. How did they go about it?
- Were the stones really responsible for the soup, or did the soldiers trick the villagers?
- If you had been in the village when the soldiers first came through, how would you have reacted?
- What is your favorite type of soup? Why?
- What lesson did you learn from the story? (the importance of sharing)

Ideas and Activities

- Ask your family and friends what their favorite types of soup are.

- Have a stone soup party. Either follow the recipe shown below and ask guests to bring one of the ingredients, or provide a broth and have guests bring any type of vegetables to add. If you decide to add a stone, make sure to remove it before you really serve the soup. While the soup is simmering, read **Stone Soup**.

Stone Soup

Ingredients: 2 large clean, uncracked round stones (optional), 1 lb. (456.6 g) stew beef (optional), 2 medium onions, 4 large carrots, 1/2 cup (125 mL) barley, 6 cups (1.5 L) water, salt and pepper to taste, 1/4 cup (63 mL) oil, 1 cup (250 mL) sliced celery, 1 cup (250 mL) peeled and cubed potatoes, 1 large can tomatoes

Directions: Peel and chop the onions and carrots. Set these aside. Cut the stew meat into small pieces and then brown it in hot oil. Add the chopped vegetables and water. Bring the soup to a boil. Turn down the heat and simmer it until the meat is tender, approximately 1 hour. Add the barley and salt and pepper to taste. Cook about 1/2 hour or until the barley is tender. Serve.

- Read another version of **Stone Soup**. Compare the stories and characters.

Related Reading

Johnston, Tony. **The Stone Bone.** Harcourt Brace and Company, 1990.

McGovern, Ann. **Stone Soup.** Scholastic, 1986.

Stewig, John W. **Stone Soup.** Holiday House, 1991.

Van Rynback, Iris, ed. **The Stone Soup.** Greenwillow Books, 1988.

Strega Nona

Retold and Illustrated by Tomie dePaola

Prentice Hall, 1975

Summary

Strega Nona is a "grandmother witch" in Calabria. She has magical powers. This makes everyone except Big Anthony stay away from her. He answers her ad asking for someone to help around her house. One evening, he overhears Strega Nona singing a magic spell. However, Big Anthony gets called in for supper and doesn't see her finish the spell. Merriment ensues when Strega Nona visits a friend and leaves Big Anthony in charge. As Big Anthony tries casting a magic spell, he learns a lesson which is sure to affect his appetite.

Hints for Reading Aloud

For some children, **Strega Nona** will be too long to listen to in one sitting. Gauge your child's ability to pay attention and listen. This story has natural breaks, so you can choose a good place to stop. As you read the second page that describes Strega Nona's powers, take time to show the delightful pictures to your child. Sound like Strega Nona by raising or lowering your voice. Read Big Anthony's part with a loud voice.

According to the story, the spell for the pasta pot is actually a little song. Create your own tune or read the spell in a sing-song voice. Use the punctuation to guide you in your singing.

Shout when Big Anthony shouts, and clap when the townspeople applaud. Blow kisses when the story indicates this. Encourage your child to do the same.

What to Talk About

- What was Anthony's mistake? What lesson might be learned about listening? Ask your child what might have happened if Strega Nona hadn't returned when she did. Was the punishment that she gave to Anthony a fair one?

- Talk about other folk tales that involve magic. Stories like **The Golden Goose, Jack and the Beanstalk, Rumpelstiltskin,** and **Hansel and Gretel** are a few. Compare and contrast them to **Strega Nona**.

- Nona means grandmother in Italian. What are some common names for grandparents?

Ideas and Activities

- There are many different types of pasta on the market today. Determine which types look similar to the kind Strega Nona's pot produced. With your child, make a pot of that pasta, following the directions on the package. Before making the pasta let your child see it uncooked and then compare how it looks cooked. Depending on what type you buy, the shape may change when you cook it.

- Buy several different types of pasta, including some of the colored ones. The small pieces rather than the large strand type will work better for this activity. Give your child some white glue, markers, or pencils, and poster board. Together draw an outline of something simple like the pasta pot in the story. Then glue one type of pasta on the outline and another type to fill in the picture.

- Make up another rhyme that might have been used to make the magic pot work or stop working. On subsequent readings of the story, try your rhyme in place of Strega Nona's.

- Your child may enjoy Winnie the Witch's humorous capers, using the following computer software: **Dragons, a Fish, and a Witch** by Houghton Mifflin Interactive. CD-ROM for MAC and PC. Available from Educorp, 7434 Trade Street, San Diego, CA 92121-2410. 1-800-843-9497. In addition, you may wish to obtain a computer software version of an Italian folk tale such as **The Princess and the Crab** by Kudos. CD-ROM for MAC and WIN. Available from Davidson & Associates, P.O. Box 2961, Torrance, CA 90503. 1-800-545-7677.

Related Reading

dePaola, Tomie. **Big Anthony and the Magic Ring.** Simon and Schuster, 1982.

dePaola, Tomie. **The Mysterious Giant of Barletta: An Italian Folktale.** Harcourt, 1988.

dePaola, Tomie. **Strega Nona's Magic Lessons.** Simon and Schuster, 1982.

dePaola, Tomie. **Tony's Bread: An Italian Folktale.** Putnam, 1989.

Manson, Christopher. **The Crab Prince.** Henry Holt, 1991.

Stevens, Janet (Reteller) **Androcles and the Lion.** Holiday, 1989.

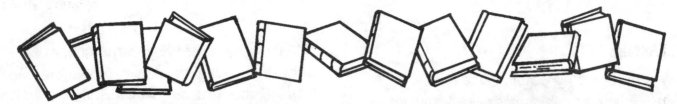

Sylvester and the Magic Pebble

Written and Illustrated by William Steig

Simon and Schuster, 1969

Summary

Sylvester, a young donkey who lives with his mother and father, enjoys collecting rocks. One day Sylvester finds a bright red pebble which turns out to be magic. Whatever Sylvester wishes for comes true as long as he is touching the pebble. He hurries toward home to let his parents know they can have whatever they wish. Frightened by a lion, Sylvester is turned into a rock, and the pebble is dropped two feet away. He lies in a field for many months. His frantic parents are heartbroken. By a lucky accident, Sylvester's parents help him turn back into a donkey. They put the lucky pebble away, realizing they now have everything they want.

Hints for Reading Aloud

Make Sylvester sound overjoyed when he realizes that the pebble is magical. Have him sound very sad when he is a prisoner inside the rock. His parents should be extremely unhappy when looking for Sylvester. Emphasize both the sad words—"dreadful," "miserable," "hopeless," as well as the happy ones—"lucky," "embraces," and "kisses."

What to Talk About

- Ask why Sylvester is so happy when he finds the magic pebble.

- Explain how the ending shows that this family does not need a magic pebble to be happy. Perhaps you will want to tell your child that love cannot be found with a magic pebble, and it cannot be bought with money. Let your child know that your feelings for her or him are just as strong as Sylvester's parents' are for their son. If your child is old enough to understand a "moral," explain that the writer wanted to have readers understand the meaning of love and happiness.

Ideas and Activities

- Find a Disney video or other cartoon with talking animals. Compare the way the film animals act with the action of the characters characters in **Sylvester and the Magic Pebble** and other talking animal books your child likes.

- If you have a pet, watch it for a while and look for ways in which it acts almost human. Do the two of you agree that your pet is thinking real thoughts? What are those thoughts? You might have your child draw a picture of your pet. Then show how animals talk in newspaper comics. Draw some dialogue balloons over the picture your child drew. Fill the balloons with words your child believes your pet is thinking.

- Find a local zoo or farm that has horses and donkeys. Point out differences in the way the two act and look. Can your child state similarities between the two animals? Which does your child like better?

- Start a rock collection with your child. You may want to collect a certain shape or color of rock. A memorable collection is one where you find a rock on each trip that you take together. Just make sure to bring some plastic bags for packing the rocks. When you get home, you can use a hot glue gun to attach them to index cards or poster board, depending on how large they are. Label each one with the place and the date you found it.

- Paint a rock. Smooth stones are best. Make sure the rock is clean and dry. Then use tempera paint to decorate it. Some markers may also work.

Related Reading

Holl, Coby. **Niki's Little Donkey.** North-South, 1993.

Steig, William. **Farmer Palmer's Wagon Ride.** Farrar, 1992.

Steig, William. **Gorky Rises.** Farrar, 1986.

Steig, William. **Roland the Minstrel Pig.** Farrar, 1968.

Steig, William. **Solomon and the Rusty Nail.** Farrar, 1985.

Steig, William. **Tiffky Doofky.** Farrar, 1978.

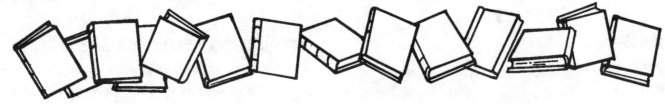

Tacky the Penguin

Written by Helen Lester

Illustrated by Lynn Munsinger

Houghton Mifflin, 1988

Summary

"Tacky was an odd bird." This sentence from the book about a funny little penguin sums up Tacky the Penguin. While Tacky's penguin companions are all neat, orderly, and they sing on key, Tacky is an odd critter who is not well accepted by his peers. But Tacky's wits save him and the other penguins from the hunters in a most humorous fashion. Tacky's companions come to accept him even if he is different from them.

Hints for Reading Aloud

While reading the narrative make sure to read each line of numbers at the part when the penguins march. Read them very precisely and evenly, spacing them when the penguins march properly. When Tacky marches, read them in a helter-skelter way—sometimes fast, sometimes slow—just as Tacky would. When you get to the "thump, thump, thump," read in a big booming voice and, with your feet, thump on the floor. Chant the hunters' song, booming out the word "RICH." Sing the song the penguins make up for the hunters. Sing it loudly and off key to any tune that pleases you. Read the last page with some acceptance in your voice.

What to Talk About

Ask your child some or all of the following questions:

- Why do you think the penguins names are Goodly, Lovely, Angel, Neatly, Perfect, and Tacky? What do their names tell you about them? Which penguin would you rather be?

- What did you think about Tacky? Why don't the penguins like him in the beginning of the story? What changes their minds?

- Is it difficult to be an individual and stand up for what you believe in? Why?

Ideas and Activities

• The penguins sing a song called "How Many Toes Does a Fish Have?"

Make up your own song to go with that title. As an alternative, sing the following song about penguins to the tune of "Have You Ever Seen a Lassie?"

Have you ever seen a
penguin, a penguin, a
penguin?
Have you ever seen a
penguin swim this way and
that?
Swim this way and that way
and this way and that way?
Have you ever seen penguin
swim this way and that?

Repeat this, substituting slide for swim; waddle for swim; and dress for swim.

• There are many types of penguins. The largest is the emperor penguin. When fully grown, it's about 4 feet (1.3 meters) high and weighs close to 100 pounds (45 kilograms). The most common is the Adele penguin. It's about 2 feet (0.6 m) high and weighs about 11 pounds (5 kilograms). What type of penguin is Tacky?

• Make a black and white mosaic using a sheet of colored paper, lots of small black and white paper squares, pencil, and glue. Together choose something that is black and white, such as a penguin. Draw an outline of it on the colored paper. Dab a bit of glue on the black and white squares and fill in the shape.

• A penguin looks like it's wearing a tuxedo. Find a picture in a book or magazine of a black and white tuxedo. See if you can name other animals that look like they're wearing human clothing. Compare pictures of the clothes and animals.

• Try marching together. First try the even rhythm of the penguins calling the numbers. Next try to march to Tacky's rhythm. Lastly, make up some marches. You can add rhythm sticks or pot lids for marchers to bang together.

• Invite family and friends to a penguin parade. Dress in black and white and waddle like a penguin. Take turns leading the parade and using different waddles.

• The other penguins greet each other politely, while Tacky is rather loud. Talk about good manners and proper greetings. Practice various forms of greetings.

• Identify the hunters. Why are these animals portrayed as the hunters?

Related Reading

Benson, Patrick. **Little Penguin.** Putnam, 1991.

Cousteau Society. **Penguins.** Simon & Schuster, 1992.

Fontanel, Beatrice. **The Penguin: A Funny Bird.** Charlesbridge, 1992.

Rigby, Rodney. **Hello, This Is Your Penguin Speaking.** Hyperion, 1992.

The Tale of Peter Rabbit

Written and Illustrated by Beatrix Potter

Frederick Warne, 1902, Penguin, 1989

Summary

Peter Rabbit is the naughty bunny in this classic tale. Warned by his mother to behave, Peter sets off on an adventure that young children will delight in hearing. Peter's trails take him through Farmer McGregor's garden. One narrow escape leads to another, and Peter ends up losing his clothes along the way. The young listener waits to find out if Peter will be able to find his way out of the garden. Peter's escapades leave him feeling out of sorts while his well-behaved siblings, Flopsy, Mopsy, and Cotton-tail, get to eat bread, milk, and blackberries.

Hints for Reading Aloud

Beatrix Potter wrote the Peter Rabbit books for small hands to hold. Let your little one hold the book as you read. (See the **Related Reading** for other titles.) On the first page, Flopsy, Mopsy, Cotton-tail, and Peter are introduced. Pause as you say each name and point to it. When you read the mother's dialogue on the next page, do it in a high-pitched tone. Think how you sound giving your own child advice, and use that tone. Later on when Mr. McGregor yells, "Stop, thief!" use a loud, authoritative voice. As you describe Peter's escape through the garden, sound hurried but do not lose clarity. When Peter sobs, make crying noises such as "Oh, oh, oh," or "Boo hoo hoo." At Peter's sneeze, make a loud sneezing sound. Make scratching noises with your nails for the hoe. Read the rest of the story with enthusiasm, finishing the last page with a flourish as you read "The End."

What to Talk About

Ask your child some or all of the following questions:

- What advice did Peter's mother give to him? Why did he disobey her?
- Has there been a time you did something you shouldn't have after being told not to? Why? What happened?
- Were you surprised by Peter's adventure? What did you think would happen to him?
- Peter's father landed in a pie. What did this mean? (Be sensitive to your child's needs. If death is not a concept you want to deal with, skip over this.)

Ideas and Activities

- There are words which may be unfamiliar. Since they are used in context, the meaning will probably be clear. Some of these include currant buns—raisin buns, similar to cinnamon buns; sieve—strainer; scarecrow—dummy placed in a garden to scare off birds; fortnight—two weeks; and chamomile tea—an herb tea.

- Plant a garden with your child. It can be a full vegetable garden if you have the space and inclination, or it can be a simple container-type garden. In limited gardening space sweet potatoes grow well in jars. Follow these simple directions: You need four toothpicks, a medium-size sweet potato, water, and a wide-mouth jar. Push the toothpicks into the sweet potato about four inches (10.5 cm) from the top. These form supports so the toothpicks can rest on the lip of the jar. Fill the jar with water and put the potato in it. Add water to the jar as needed, and watch the vine grow.

- Find out more about real bunnies. Many pet shops have them, so you can have an outing to see one close up and perhaps pet one.

- Take advantage of the many vegetables mentioned in the story to give your child an opportunity to taste them. These include lettuces (there are several types available), French beans, radishes, parsley, cucumber, cabbage, and potatoes. Cook them, as appropriate, or serve them raw. Do not overwhelm your child with these all at once, but offer small bites of each. Some kind of dip or dressing might make the first taste more enticing.

- You and your child can enjoy many Beatrix Potter stories by watching the video **Tales of Beatrix Potter Collection** (Coffee Table Video, 1986).

Related Reading

Brewster, Patience. **Rabbit Inn.** Little, 1991.

Brown, Margaret Wise. **The Runaway Bunny.** Harper, 1972.

Casely, Judith. **Grandpa's Garden Lunch.** Greenwillow, 1986.

Delton, Judy. **Hired Help for Rabbit.** Macmillan, 1992.

Dubanevich, Arlene. **Pig William.** Macmillan, 1985.

Peet, Bill. **Zella, Zach, and Zodiac.** Houghton, 1986.

Pizer, Abigail. **Charlie the Puppy.** Carolrhoda, 1989.

Potter, Beatrix. **The Complete Adventures of Peter Rabbit.** Warne, 1987.

Potter, Beatrix. **The Complete Adventures of Tom Kitten.** Puffin, 1987.

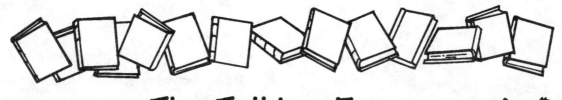

The Talking Eggs

Written by Robert D. San Souci

Illustrated by Jerry Pinkey

Scholastic, 1989

Summary

This Southern fairy tale concerns two sisters, Blanche and Rose. Blanche runs away because her mother and sister are very cruel. She meets an old woman who asks for some water. When Blanche kindly helps her, the old woman takes her home. Blanche is obedient to the old woman's requests and is rewarded with some eggs. The old woman cautions Blanche not to pick up the beautiful eggs that say, "Don't take me." Blanche follows the instructions and picks up the plain ones which cry, "Take me." On the way home, as directed, Blanche throws the eggs over her right shoulder. Lovely dresses and jewels come out of them.

Blanche's mother and sister decide to get some riches for themselves. Rose meets the old woman but refuses to do as she is instructed. She takes the beautiful "don't take me" eggs. When she throws them over her right shoulder, snakes and wolves run after her. The mother chases the animals away. Returning home, they find Blanche has gone to the city where she remains as kind as always. The mother and Rose spend the rest of their lives looking for the old woman's cabin, but it has disappeared forever.

Hints for Reading Aloud

The mother's voice should be distinctly different when speaking to her favorite daughter, Rose, than to Blanche. However, the old woman needs to sound kind to both—at least until she finds out what kind of a person Rose is. Just think of Cinderella and her wicked stepsisters when doing the voices for Blanche and Rose.

What to Talk About

- Does this book remind you of another story? If your child doesn't make the connection to **Cinderella,** give some clues. **Example:** "I am thinking of another story where there are three sisters, a nice one and two mean ones." Discuss other similarities between this tale and **Cinderella.**

- Why do you think the mother likes Rose more than Blanche? Point out the words, "They were alike as two peas in a pod." Explain what this saying means.

- The illustrations are particularly colorful here. Talk about the fanciful animals and eggs. Point out the similarity between Rose's clothes and the mother's.

Ideas and Activities

- Has your child ever tried coloring eggs? Try to duplicate one or two of the eggs shown in the illustrations. Egg coloring kits may be a bit harder to get in the fall than the spring, but a craft store should be able to help you. You can also use food coloring by following the directions on the box.

- The American South has many special cultures. Introduce your child to them. **The Talking Eggs** has a Creole feel and look. Locate a restaurant in your area that features Creole or other southern recipes. Perhaps you are familiar with the toe-tapping zydeco music. If not, get a CD, record, or tape and enjoy it with your child.

- Find a moral in this story with your child. After reading, see if your child can conclude that just because something is pretty on the outside doesn't mean it will be pretty on the inside.

- Every culture has its own fairy tales. Your child might be most familiar with the Germanic Grimm's or the French. A bookstore clerk or librarian should be able to help you find a treasure trove of tales from other lands. Some titles are given below in the **Related Reading**. The Native American, Chinese, and Indian cultures have particularly interesting stories.

Related Reading

Durrel, Ann, Selector. **The Dianne Goode Book of American Folk Tales and Songs.** Dutton, 1989.

Hunter, C.W. **The Green Gourd: A North Carolina Folktale.** Putnam, 1992.

Kellogg, Steven. **Paul Bunyan.** Morrow, 1984.

Ludwig, Warren. **Good Morning, Granny Rose.** Putnam, 1990.

Polacco, Patricia. **Rechenka's Eggs**. Putnam, 1988

San Souci, Robert D. (Reteller) **Sukey and the Mermaid.** Macmillan, 1992.

Scieszka, Jon. **The True Story of the Three Little Pigs by A. Wolf.** Viking, 1989.

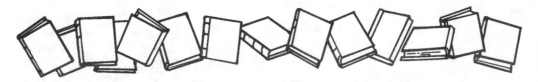

Too Many Tamales

Written by Gary Soto

Illustrated by Ed Martinez

Putnam, 1993

Summary

In this Christmas tale, Maria happily helps her mother make tamales for the family Christmas celebration. When Mama leaves to answer the telephone, Maria gives in to temptation and tries on the diamond ring her mother has left on the counter while making the tamales. It's not until the tamales are finished and the family has arrived that Maria realizes the ring is no longer on her finger. Enlisting the help of Dolores, Teresa, and Danny, Maria determines the best way to find the ring is to eat the tamales. Full tummies do not help turn up the lost ring, and Maria has to let her mother know it is missing. She discovers that Mama is wearing the ring! She realizes what happened, and the family sets off to make another batch of tamales.

Hints for Reading Aloud

Read the story with feeling. Make Maria sound a little sneaky when she decides to wear the ring. You might want to look around as if someone were watching you. When Maria screams "The ring!" make her sound alarmed. When she scolds her cousins, make her sound annoyed. Let her mother sound understanding and even a bit playful when she realizes what Maria has done and that more tamales need to be made.

What to Talk About

- Ask your child why Maria wanted to try on the ring. Should she have done so without asking her mother's permission?

- How could Maria have handled the situation in a different way?

- Ask your child if she or he would have eaten the tamales to help Maria out?

- Have you or your child ever eaten so much you didn't feel well? Why do you think you ate that much?

Ideas and Activities

- You may wish to make tamales from scratch with your child. This is a complex process and will require lots of patience. You can find a recipe in a Mexican cookbook. Masa, the special corn flour, is with the baking goods or foreign foods in many grocery stores. Cornhusks may be found with the spices. Make sure you read the recipe carefully and have everything ready before you start. Tamales can be made with all kinds of fillings, from meats to sweets. If you prefer, you can buy tamales that are already prepared.

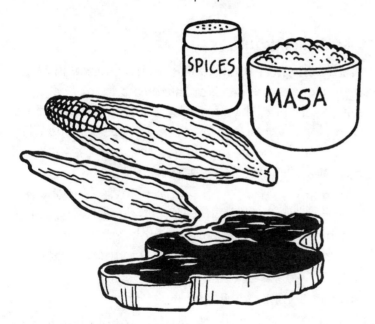

- In this story, Maria's family comes to her home and eats tamales at Christmas. What special foods does your family associate with holidays? Enlist your child's help in making one of these treats.

- The children in the story cut out pictures that are in the newspaper of things they hope will be under the Christmas tree. Let your child make a "picture list." If your child is very young, show pictures of various items and have her or him point to the ones desired. Help your child tear out or cut out those pictures. Glue them onto a sheet of paper. You can write the name of each item under its picture. Older children can do the whole process by themselves.

- The family in the story makes tamales together. Let your family come up with an activity that will become a family holiday tradition. It might be a cooking project, making name cards and place mats, or singing songs together.

- The masa in the tamales must be kneaded. This age-old baking technique is a stimulating motor skill for children. Use real dough or clay. It is just a matter of patting out and then rolling up the dough again and again.

Related Reading

Demarest, Chris L. **No Peas for Nellie.** Macmillan, 1988.

dePaola, Tomie. **Pancakes for Breakfast.** Harcourt, 1978.

Engel, Diana. **Gino Badino.** Morrow, 1991.

Mahy, Margaret. **Jam: A True Story.** Little, 1986.

Polacco, Patricia. **Thunder Cake.** Putnam, 1990.

Shelby, Anne. **Potluck.** Orchard, 1991.

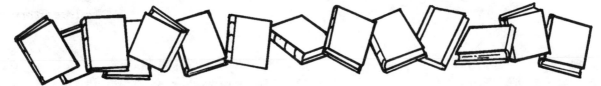

The True Story of the Three Little Pigs

Written by A. Wolf as told to Jon Scieszka

Illustrated by Lane Smith

Viking Children's Books, 1992.

Summary

This is the familiar story of the three little pigs told from the wolf's point of view. It seems that when the wolf went to the doors of the three pigs' houses, all he wanted was a cup of sugar to finish a cake for his grandmother's birthday. At each door, he was overcome by a sneeze which just happened to demolish the houses of the first two pigs. Since the pigs were already dead, he ate them for dinner. (As A. Wolf says, "Think of it as a big cheeseburger just lying there.") At the last pig's house, the wolf is arrested by the police and thrown in jail. There he stays, a victim of prejudice against wolves.

Hints for Reading Aloud

This is a very funny book, but it is for a child with a well-developed sense of humor. A younger child might find it frightening since in the traditional story the first two pigs are saved by the last one who lives in the brick house. This book has the wolf eating the first two pigs.

Make the wolf sound very kind at the door of the pigs' houses. Remember he is "telling" this story, so he is making himself sound innocent. The last pig should sound mean and nasty—just like the wolf might sound in the conventional story.

What to Talk About

- Ask why the wolf sounds like a kind animal in this story. How is this version different from the traditional one? If your child is not familiar with the conventional version, get a copy of it—or the Disney cartoon—so she or he will understand and appreciate the humor of Scieszka's parody.

- Is the wolf's story an honest one? Why or why not? Is the wolf really "big and bad"? Discuss how the wolf's sneezing is a different way of looking at the destruction of the pigs' houses from the original telling of the story.

- Point out the humor in the illustrations. Have your child notice the handkerchief the wolf carries. What design is on the handkerchief? How is the second pig pictured after his house is destroyed? Point out the articles in "The Daily Pig" newspaper.

Ideas and Activities

- This version of the story is often used to teach students about point of view. Point of view is the narrator's opinion or attitude about the subject. The story has previously been told by a narrator who was sympathetic to the pigs. However, this one has just the opposite point of view. Think of other books that have a villain and ask how the story might be different if it was told by the "bad guy." An example could be **Cinderella** as told by the stepmother or one of the stepsisters. How would they describe how Cinderella was treated? How might they talk about what happened at the Prince's ball? If your child is ready to think about literature in this way, she or he will enjoy retelling other stories.

- Some children have a wonderfully developed sense of humor. If your child is one of these, locate other humorous books in the library. Show your child that some books can make the reader laugh out loud. A children's librarian can help you find these selections. Also, check out joke books. Children usually love to tell jokes, and you can enjoy these together. Introduce "knock-knock" jokes and other riddles.

- Find out more about pigs and wolves. Read encyclopedias or other nonfiction books and decide if the two are predator and prey.

- Read a traditional version of this age-old fairy tale. Compare this book with the traditional version. See the suggestions in **Related Reading**.

- Think about the pigs' houses. Explore the different types of materials used to build houses. Build a house together, using building blocks or playing cards.

- One of the traditional versions on video is **My Favorite Fairy Tales: The Three Little Pigs** (Hi-Tops Video, 1986). For a heartwarming pig story, watch the video of **Babe** (MCA Home Video, 1996).

Related Reading

Galdone, Paul. **The Three Little Pigs.** Houghton Mifflin, 1979.

Hooks, William H. **The Three Little Pigs and the Fox.** Dial, 1989.

Marshall, James. **The Three Little Pigs.** Dial, 1989.

Quackenbush, Robert. **Robert Quackenbush's Treasury of Humor.** Doubleday, 1992.

Scieszka, Jon. **The Frog Prince, Continued.** Viking, 1991.

Zamach, Harve. **The Three Little Pigs: An Old Story.** Farrar, Strauss, & Giroux, 1989.

Tuesday

Written and Illustrated by David Wiesner

Clarion Books, 1991

Summary

This practically wordless book shows the Tuesday evening when frogs from a pond begin to fly toward town on their lily pads. Their adventures include seeing a man having a late snack, gliding through a clothesline, watching a bit of television, and chasing a confused dog. The police are confounded by the lily pads left in the street after the frogs hop back into the pond. Everything is normal until the next Tuesday evening when some pigs begin to rise up from the barnyard.

Hints for Reading Aloud

Here is a book that you and your child can read. You might start by letting him or her turn the pages, without commenting on what is shown in the book. No doubt your child will be delighted by the adventures. The second time

through have your little one notice the expressions on the frogs' faces as they watch TV or chase the dog. Point out the poor frog who is just about covered by the linen as he passes under the clothesline.

What to Talk About

- Show your child that the frogs are not all the same. Some are brown, and the markings are quite different. There are a few pictures where you can show the differences in the lily pads, too.

- Your child will want to see that the man in the robe being interviewed by the TV reporters is the same one having his late night snack as the frog flew by his window. Also, does your child think the dog sniffing the lily pads is the same one that is chased by the frog?

- What sort of expression does the detective have on his face when he holds the lily pad with his pencil?

Ideas and Activities

- Does your child think your family's pet (or the neighbor's) might have a secret life when humans are not watching it? What does that pet do all day long when no one is home? What does it do at night when everyone else is asleep? Create your own story.

- Your child might be interested in the life cycle of a frog. You might want to raise some from tadpoles. This may be a nice time to introduce your child to tadpoles if these creatures are not already familiar. Get some illustrated books from the library. Try to find a pet store or zoo where your child can see tadpoles, as well as different types of adult frogs.

- Ask your child whether human beings can fly. Talk about airplanes and hot-air balloons. What would it be like to see a human being flying down the street without any type of machine? If you have a place in your community where hang gliders soar, you might take your child to see them. This is probably the closest human beings will ever come to flying.

- **Tuesday** ends with some pigs beginning their adventure. What might happen to these pigs as they reach the town? Would they be able to do the same things that the frogs did? Talk about what special adventures those pigs might have. Invite your child to draw a picture of a pig flying through your neighborhood.

Related Reading

Jackson, Ellen. **Ants Can't Dance.** Macmillan, 1991.

McMillan, Bruce. **The Remarkable Riderless Runaway Tricycle.** Apple Island, 1985.

Sadler, Marilyn. **Alistair Underwater.** Simon & Schuster, 1990.

Solotareff, Gregoire. **The Ogre and the Frog King.** Greenwillow, 1988.

Teague, Mark. **Frog Medicine.** Scholastic, 1991.

Vesey, A. **The Princess and the Frog.** Little, 1985.

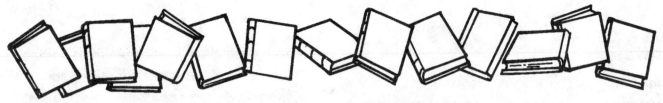

A Turkey for Thanksgiving

Written by Eve Bunting

Illustrated by Diane deGroat

Clarion Books, 1991

Summary

Mr. and Mrs. Moose are getting ready for their Thanksgiving feast. They have invited all their friends. Mrs. Moose longs for a turkey, so Mr. Moose sets out to find one. He is joined on his search by Rabbit, the Goats, Sheep, and Porcupine. They arrive at Turkey's nest where a posted sign declares, "Do Not Disturb! (Come back after Thanksgiving.)" Turkey runs but is no match for Mr. Moose. Turkey is dragged back to Mrs. Moose. She is delighted and immediately sets a place for Turkey, who is even more delighted and very relieved. Mrs. Moose says how nice it is to have friends around the table. Turkey declares, "It's even nicer to be AT your table and not ON it. Happy Thanksgiving, everybody."

Hints for Reading Aloud

This story has fine opportunities for you to create animal talking sounds. Try to have each animal voice sound unique. Mr. and Mrs. Moose might have loud and deep voices, while Rabbit could have a high-pitched voice. Porcupine might be shy and the Goats boisterous. The turkey will, of course, sound relieved as the chair is brought for it. Your child might suggest how each would sound. Perhaps she or he will want to make the "real" animal sound as each is introduced in the story.

What to Talk About

- You'll want to discuss why the turkey is so scared when found by Mr. Moose and then so happy at the end. Your child might understand that the spirit of Thanksgiving is not about what we eat but rather about having friends and relatives spend the day with us. Ask who he or she is looking forward to seeing at Thanksgiving this year.

Ideas and Activities

• This story might be your child's first introduction to the Thanksgiving holiday. Find a book in the children's section of the library which relates the beginnings of the holiday. It might be surprising to find that the day was not designated as a national holiday until Abraham Lincoln's administration. It was moved around in November until Franklin D. Roosevelt said it would always be on the fourth Thursday.

• Thanksgiving lends itself to all sorts of decorations, and your child might want to try drawing a turkey. Make handprint turkeys. Trace your hand and your child's hand onto a large piece of paper. Then color in a face on the thumb, and make the fingers into the turkey's tail feathers. This is an enjoyable holiday activity that will keep children amused. The handprint turkeys can serve as place mats.

• Your child may be old enough to relate some of the reasons why she or he is thankful. Have your youngster recount some as you write them down. Ask your child to illustrate the reasons and show this work to the whole family before the big Thanksgiving meal.

• What is your family's traditional Thanksgiving meal? While a large number of people eat turkey, there are many who do not. For instance, vegetarians do not eat turkey. Find out what others consider Thanksgiving dinner to be.

• Create a whimiscal imaginary Thanksgiving menu with your child. Try things like marvelous mashed potatoes and truly tantalizing turkey.

Related Reading

Dalgliesh, Alice. **The Thanksgiving Story.** Macmillan, 1988.

Kroll, Steven. **Oh, What a Thanksgiving.** Scholastic, 1988.

Raphael, Elaine, and Don Bolognese. **The Story of the First Thanksgiving.** Scholastic, 1991.

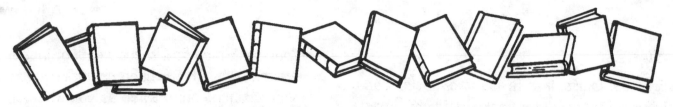

Two Bad Ants

Written and Illustrated by Chris Van Allsburg

Houghton Mifflin, 1988

Summary

After bringing a sugar crystal to their queen, the ants in a colony are told to bring more. They slowly move toward the house and sugar bowl. Two of the ants decide it would be better to live in the place where the crystal comes from than to go back and forth between the bowl and their home. However, they soon find this new residence is a dangerous place to be. During their adventures, they are drenched by coffee, almost swallowed by a human, have a hot time in the toaster, and experience an electrifying moment in the outlet. Later, these two ants see their fellow ants returning for more crystals and happily join them for the trip back to their original home. Since the narrator of this story is an ant, none of the human names for objects are used.

Hints for Reading Aloud

Emphasize the verbs in the story. Ants are constantly on the move, and the action words will demonstrate this to your child. Words like "climbed," "marched," and "crawled" especially explain ant movement. You might point out how "climbed" is used at different times in the story.

What to Talk About

- Have your child name the different places the ants go. Explain that these ants have never been in a house before, so they are not familiar with the different objects they find there. When they are caught in the garbage disposal, it can only be described as "a whirling storm of shredded food and stinging rain." As you talk about the different objects in the house, you might show your child why the author/narrator describes them in this special way.

- Talk about the title. Does your child think these ants are bad? Who might call them "bad"? Most readers would probably say they were curious. What is your child curious about? Remind your youngster of the last time he or she was doing something out of curiosity that you thought was dangerous.

Ideas and Activities

- Has your child ever had an ant farm? This might be an interesting hobby. Discuss how the behavior of ants is similar to those shown in this book.

- Perhaps your child would like to describe a favorite toy as seen through the eyes of an ant crawling on it. Is it round or square? Does it have jagged edges like a leaf, or is it smooth like a street? Is it as soft as sand or as hard as a rock?

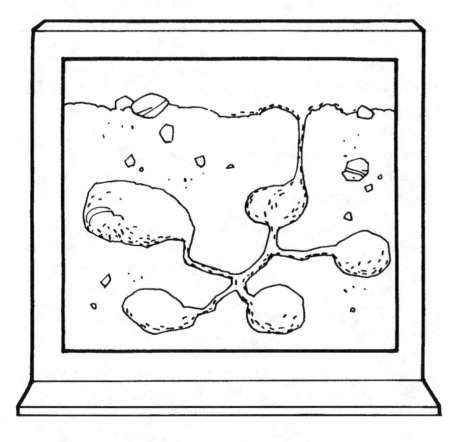

- Children often find the subject of insects more exciting than adults do. Find some information about them at your library. You may be able to find a book with magnified pictures of insects. Zoos often have areas where insects are kept. Check this out together.

- The ants wind up in the sugar bowl. With your child take a spoonful of sugar and examine it closely. What does it look like? Put the sugar onto a piece of waxed paper. Spread it around. Do you notice any differences? Try looking at it one more time using a magnifying glass. Does it look any different now?

- Ants are very small creatures. With your child imagine what it would be like to be as small as an ant. Make a list of all the things you might be able to do that you can't do now.

Related Reading

Chinery, Michael. **Ant.** (Series: **Life Story**) Troll, 1990.

Dorros, Arthur. **Ant City.** Harper, 1987.

Fisher, Aileen. **When It Comes to Bugs: Poems.** Harper, 1986.

Sabin, Francene. **Amazing World of Ants.** Troll, 1982.

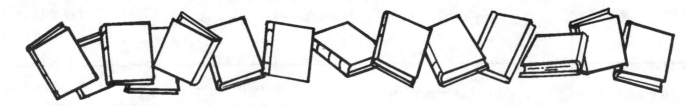

The Year at Maple Hill Farm

Written and Illustrated by Alice and Martin Provensen

Aladdin, 1978

Summary

This beautiful book describes the year on a farm, beginning with the month of January and taking the reader through every season. It is a fine book to introduce the change of seasons to children, especially for those who don't live in cold climates where the seasons tend to be more clearly defined. Animals, insects, and birds are described in the same simple but effective terms as life on the farm. This is especially helpful for children who are not familiar with the constant work it takes to live on a farm.

Hints for Reading Aloud

This book is narrative only, so there are no voices for interaction. However, the story is written in two sections. On most pages, across the top there is a story written in large text. This is the major point on the page. Lower on the page, there are lots of details about what is happening on the farm. Depending on the age and interest of your child, you might read only one part or the other, or you may wish to mix the two.

What to Talk About

- Ask your child how the seasons affect our lives. You might have to provide some helpful reminders, such as pointing out that our clothes change. How are animals on a farm affected by seasonal changes?

- If you have pets, talk about how you have to care for them. Is this similar to taking care of animals on a farm?

- What was your favorite animal on the farm? Why?

- If you live on a farm, how is the farm shown in this book similar to yours?

Ideas and Activities

- Make a weather calendar with your child. Draw a grid of 35 squares. Make one grid for each month of the year. This can be done using a computer program, drawing on a piece of paper, or folding a piece of paper seven times horizontally and 5 times vertically. Jot down the days of the week and decide how to mark the calendar to record the weather. You can draw a sun for a sunny day, some raindrops for rain, and a snowflake for the snow. If you prefer, you can purchase weather stickers for this activity. Help your child see patterns in the weather.

- Create a farm. Get cardboard tubes, small gift boxes, various colors of construction paper, glue, scissors, and magazine pictures of animals. For instance, cut a pond out of blue construction paper and use a box to create a barn. Glue the cardboard tubes to the backs of the animals so they can stand. You can, of course, add any small toy animals or vehicles to your farm. If you want to represent the farm at a different time of year, cover it with cotton balls to represent snow.

- Make some paper bag animal puppets for the different farm animals. If your child is very young, just have her or him color the animal's face on a lunch bag. If your child is older, you may want to use construction paper, glue, and scissors to make this a little more sophisticated. Make your own puppet and have a puppet show with the animals. You may want to tell riddles and jokes using your puppets.

- Talk about baby animals and what they are called. See the chart on page 39 for more information.

- Learn about farm animals, using the following software: **The New Katie's Farm** by Lawrence Productions. CD-ROM for MAC and PC. Available from Educorp, 7434 Trade Street, San Diego, CA 92121-2410. 1-800-843-9497.

Related Reading

Garland, Michael. **Michael Katie.** Harper, 1989.

Lester, Allison. **My Farm.** Houghton Mifflin, 1994.

Lindberg, Reeve. **Benjamin's Barn.** Dial, 1990.

Lindberg, Reeve. **There's a Cow on the Road!** Dial, 1993.

Martin, Bill, Jr., and John Archambault. **Barn Dance!** Lothrop, 1988.

Martin, Jacqueline Briggs. **Good Times on Grandfather Mountain.** Orchard, 1992.

Pearson, Susan. **Well, I Never!** Simon and Schuster, 1990.

Sendak, Maurice. **Chicken Soup with Rice: A Book of Months.** Harper, 1992.

Waddell, Martin. **Farmer Duck.** Candlewick, 1992.

How to Make Books with Children

Making books with children is an activity that is lots of fun for everyone involved. Books that you make with your children will be ones that they will want to read over and over again. Homemade books also make attractive gifts for family members and friends. Not only can your children present the books, they can also read them aloud to the recipients. But the best thing about making books with your children is that it brings you together in a creative way.

How long should the book be?

The age of your child will dictate how much text you will put in your book. In many cases, you will do all the writing while your child does the art. Letting your child dictate a story to you is one way to help build vocabulary. When you read the story aloud, your child will make the connection between what has been said and what has been written. It is a painless way to help your child begin the process of learning to read.

What should go in your book?

The answer is really anything you want. Throughout **Read to Me! Read to Me!** there are suggestions for making books with your child. Any of these can be used to make books. You can also make books using photographs, pictures from magazines and newspapers, postcards, and cereal boxes. The possibilities are endless. You are limited only by the ability and interest of your child and the materials you have available.

Some suggestions for different types of books follow on pages 151 and 152. Use any of them that seem to fit you and your child's needs, moods, and interests.

Here is a general list of materials that you will need to make books.

- a variety of sizes, colors, and types of paper
- poster board
- safety scissors
- adult scissors
- stapler
- glue
- pencils
- pens
- markers
- crayons
- cellophane tape
- wide electrical or duct tape
- metal book rings
- hole punch
- yarn
- ruler

150

How to Make Books with Children *(cont.)*

The Easiest Book

The easiest book to make is one where you take a few sheets of white copier paper and place one piece of construction paper on the front and one on the back. Then staple it along the left-hand side. Add anything you want inside the cover. You can also do this to create books from artwork that is not part of anything else.

Accordion Books

To make this type of book, you will need butcher paper or copier paper, cardboard or tagboard, writing paper, and crayons or markers. Fold the paper in half lengthwise for strength. Divide the fold of the paper into an even number of sections. Insert a piece of tagboard or cardboard into each end to make the book stand up on the correct side. Glue the pages to each section of the accordion book.

Panel Books

A panel book uses large sheets of construction paper. Write one page of the story on each panel. Illustrate it. You can then place the panels side by side and read the story. When you are finished, you can bind it and read it again.

Shape Books

These books are cut out in the shape of anything you choose. You use a simple shape, such as a triangle, and cut several sheets of paper into that shape. If you are reading a book about shapes, you might want to cut each page into a different shape.

If you want to make books that are the shapes of objects, such as a barn, find a picture and sketch it or trace it. Just remember to make the outline dark and large so it is easy to cut out. You can make several pages like that once you have created a template. Staple or use yarn to bind the book.

How to Make Books with Children *(cont.)*

Big Books

These are often used in schools so that many children may see the story at one time. Children at home love to help create these books. It might be that the size excites the children. For these books use large sheets of paper such as 11" x 17" (28 cm x 43 cm). You can draw large pictures and write a few words on the bottom, cut out pictures from magazines, or enlarge any picture or pattern. You can bind these books in several ways. Make sure to leave a blank page for the cover. Invite your child to write his or her name on the cover and decorate it.

1. Staple the story pages together. Cover the staples with tape so fingers won't get cut.

2. Punch holes along the side of the book. If you punch three holes, you can add yarn or metal book rings to keep your book together. You may wish to use hole reinforcements for the holes you punch.

3. If you have created several separate pages, you might want to try another method of binding that works especially well with big books. Tape the left side of the back page to a tabletop. Working from the back to the front of the book, add and tape down each page to the left side. Lift up all the pages and fold the tape edges around the back page. Cover the binding with strong, wide tape. You might want to use electrical or duct tape for this step.

Little Books

Just as children love big books, they also love little books to carry around. To make one you will need butcher or copier paper, scissors, and crayons or markers. Below are the directions.

1. Fold the paper to make eight boxes.

2. Fold the paper in half, and cut a slit to the first fold only.

3. Open up the sheets and fold along the long fold. Push both ends toward the middle.

4. Keep pushing in until the middle portion is flat. Fold the side over in the same direction to complete the little book.

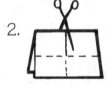
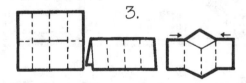
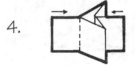

Caldecott Award Books

The Caldecott medal was established in 1938. It is a medal that is presented annually by the American Library Association to the illustrator of the most distinguished American picture book for children published in the United States in the preceding year. The winner must be a resident or citizen of the United States. These books actually make excellent read-aloud selections because the illustrations and the text are of such high quality. They have lasting appeal, and most are still in print.

Year	Illustrator	Book
1997	David Wisniewski	*Golem*
1996	Peggy Rathmann	*Officer Buckle and Gloria*
1995	David Diaz	*Smoky Night* (Text: Eve Bunting)
1994	Allen Say	*Grandfather's Journey*
1993	Emily Arnold McCully	*Mirette on the High Wire*
1992	David Wiesner	*Tuesday*
1991	David Macauley	*Black and White*
1990	Ed Young	*Lon Po Po:* *A Red Riding Hood Story from China*
1989	Stephen Gammell	*Song and Dance Man* (Text: Karen Ackerman)
1988	John Schoenherr	*Owl Moon* (Text: Jane Yolen)
1987	Richard Egielski	*Hey, Al* (Text: Arthur Yorinks)
1986	Chris Van Allsburg	*The Polar Express*
1985	Trina Schart Hyman	*Saint George and the Dragon* (Text: Margaret Hodges)
1984	Alice and Martin Provensen	*The Glorious Flight:* *Across the Channel with Louis Bleriot*
1983	Marcia Brown	*Shadow* (Text: Blaise Cendrars)
1982	Chris Van Allsburg	*Jumanji*
1981	Arnold Lobel	*Fables*
1980	Barbara Cooney	*Ox-Cart Man* (Text: Donald Hall)

Caldecott Award Books *(cont.)*

Year	Illustrator	Book
1979	Paul Goble	*The Girl Who Loved Wild Horses*
1978	Peter Spier	*Noah's Ark* (Text: Jacob Revius)
1977	Leo and Diane Dillon	*Ashanti to Zulu: African Traditions* (Text: Margaret Musgrove)
1976	Leo and Diane Dillon	*Why Mosquitoes Buzz in People's Ears: A West African Tale* (Text: Verna Aardema)
1975	Gerald McDermott	*Arrow to the Sun: A Pueblo Indian Tale*
1974	Margo Zemack	*Duffy and the Devil* (Text: Harve Zemach)
1973	Blair Lent	*The Funny Little Woman* (Text: Arlene Mosel)
1972	Nonny Hogrogian	*One Fine Day*
1971	Gail E. Haley	*A Story—A Story*
1970	William Steig	*Sylvester and the Magic Pebble*
1969	Uri Shulevitz	*The Fool of the World and the Flying Ship* (Text: Arthur Ransome)
1968	Ed Emberley	*Drummer Hoff* (Text: Barbara Emberley)
1967	Evaline Ness	*Sam, Bangs & Moonshine*
1966	Nonny Hogrogian	*Always Room for One More* (Text: Sorche Nic Leodhas)
1965	Beni Montresor	*May I Bring a Friend?* (Text: Beatrice Schenk de Regniers)
1964	Maurice Sendak	*Where the Wild Things Are*
1963	Ezra Jack Keats	*The Snowy Day*
1962	Marcia Brown	*Once a Mouse*
1961	Nicolas Sidjakov	*Baboushka and the Three Kings* (Text: Ruth Robbins)
1960	Marie Hall Ets	*Nine Days to Christmas* (Text: Marie Hall Ets and Aurora Labstida)

Caldecott Award Books *(cont.)*

Year	Illustrator	Book
1959	Barbara Cooney	*Chanticleer and the Fox* (Text: adapted from Geoffrey Chaucer)
1958	Robert McCloskey	*Time of Wonder*
1957	Marc Simon	*A Tree Is Nice* (Text: Janice Udry)
1956	Feodor Rojankovsky	*Frog Went A-Courtin'* (Text: John Langstaff)
1955	Marcia Brown	*Cinderella or The Little Glass Slipper* (Text: Charles Perrault)
1954	Ludwig Bemelmans	*Madeline's Rescue*
1953	Lynd K. Ward	*The Biggest Bear*
1952	Nicholas Mordvinoff	*Finders Keepers* (Text: William Lipkind)
1951	Katherine Milhous	*The Egg Tree*
1950	Leo Politi	*Song of the Swallows*
1949	Berta and Elmer Hader	*The Big Snow*
1948	Roger Duvoisin	*White Snow, Bright Snow* (Text: Alvin Tresselt)
1947	Leonard Weisgard	*The Little Island* (Text: Golden MacDonald [Margaret Wise Brown])
1946	Maud and Miska Petersham	*The Rooster Crows*
1945	Elizabeth Orton Jones	*Prayer for a Child* (Text: Rachel Field)
1944	Louis Slobodkin	*Many Moons* (Text: James Thurber)
1943	Virginia Lee Burton	*The Little House*
1942	Robert McCloskey	*Make Way for Ducklings*
1941	Robert Lawson	*They Were Strong and Good*
1940	Ingri and Edgar Parin d'Aulaire	*Abraham Lincoln*
1939	Thomas Handforth	*Mei Li*
1938	Dorothy P. Lathrop	*Animals of the Bible*

Beginning Chapter Books

Before you know it, your child will be reading independently and finding many of the books that you once read aloud no longer enjoyable to listen to. This does not and should not signal the end of your reading together. You will, however, need to do some adjusting. Find some chapter books that both of you will enjoy and read these. You might find that you can read a few pages at a time or your child will be so enthralled that you read whole chapters during one sitting. It might even work well if you read a chapter and then ask your child to read the next one.

Some of the titles suggested on this page will help you get started with chapter books that you both might feel are good ones to read together. The list includes both classics and very popular titles. If in doubt about what to read, you may wish to consult the Newbery Award list. This is generally found at public libraries and most bookstores. These books have been selected by the American Library Association as the most distinguished contribution to American children's literature published in the United States.

Adam of the Road by Elizabeth Janet Gray (Viking, 1970)

Bridge to Terabithia by Katherine Paterson (Avon, 1977)

Bunnicula: A Rabbit Tale of Mystery by Deborah and James Howe (Avon, 1979)

Caddie Woodlawn by Carol Ryrie Brink (Macmillan, 1962)

Charlotte's Web by E. B. White (HarperCollins, 1952)

The Children's Book of Virtues by William J. Bennett (Simon and Schuster, 1995)

The Cricket in Times Square by George Selden (Dell, 1960)

Follow My Leader by James B. Garfield (Viking, 1994)

A Gathering of Days: A New England Girl's Journal by Joan W. Blos (Atheneum, 1979)

How to Eat Fried Worms by Thomas Rockwell (Dell, 1973)

In the Year of the Boar and Jackie Robinson by Bette Boa Lord (HarperCollins, 1984)

James and the Giant Peach by Roald Dahl (Viking, 1961)

Maniac Magee by Jerry Spinelli (Little, Brown, 1990)

Matilda by Roald Dahl (Viking, 1988)

Mr. Popper's Penguins by Richard and Florence Atwater (Dell Yearling, 1938)

Mrs. Frisby and the Rats of NIMH by Robert C. O'Brien (Atheneum, 1971)

Old Yeller by Fred Gipson (HarperCollins, 1965)

Sarah, Plain and Tall by Patricia MacLachlan (HarperCollins, 1985)

The Secret Garden by Frances Hodgson Burnett (Dell, 1986)

Shiloh by Phyllis Reynolds Naylor (Dell Yearling, 1991)

Sounder by William H. Armstrong (HarperCollins, 1969)

Stuart Little by E. B. White (HarperCollins, 1945)

The Twenty-One Balloons by William Pene Du Bois (Dell, 1975)

The Little House Series by Laura Ingalls Wilder (published by HarperCollins)

The American Girl Series by various authors (published by Pleasant Company)

The Goosebumps Series by R.L. Stine (published by Scholastic, Inc.)

Big Books and Predictable Books

Big Books

Many of the stories described in **Read to Me! Read to Me!** are also available in Big Book format.

- Bread, Bread, Bread
- Caps for Sale
- Corduroy
- Curious George
- The Day Jimmy's Boa Ate the Wash
- Franklin in the Dark
- The Gingerbread Boy
- Goodnight Moon
- The Grouchy Ladybug
- How Much Is a Million?
- If You Give a Mouse a Cookie
- Madeline
- Make Way for Ducklings
- Mama, Do You Love Me?
- The Mitten
- The Ox-Cart Man
- School Days
- Stone Soup
- Strega Nona
- The Tale of Peter Rabbit

Predictable Books

The following stories described in **Read to Me! Read to Me!** use repetition which allows children to predict what will come next. This feature makes them especially enjoyable for youngsters.

- Brown Bear, Brown Bear
- Caps for Sale
- Chicka Chicka Boom Boom
- Chicken Little
- The Day Jimmy's Boa Ate the Wash
- The Gingerbread Boy
- Goodnight Moon
- Gregory, the Terrible Eater
- The Grouchy Ladybug
- If You Give a Mouse a Cookie
- The Little Engine That Could
- Love You Forever
- Madeline
- Millions of Cats
- Peek-A-Boo!
- Q Is for Duck

Index

The literature selections that appear in this book can be found in the index. They often overlap the various categories.

Index (cont.)

Index (cont.)